"IN YOUR JOURNEY LIES YOUR AWAKENING"

From the time you were born until now, your journey began.

DR. SHIRLEY M. GAINES

Copyright © 2013 by Dr. Shirley M. Gaines

"*In Your Journey Lies Your Awakening*"
From the time you were born until now, your journey began.
by Dr. Shirley M. Gaines

Printed in the United States of America

ISBN 9781628394634

All rights reserved solely by the author. The author guarantees all contents are original and do not infringe upon the legal rights of any other person or work. No part of this book may be reproduced in any form without the permission of the author. The views expressed in this book are not necessarily those of the publisher.

Unless otherwise indicated, Bible quotations are taken from the King James Version of the Bible. Copyright © 2007 by B. B. Kirkbride Bible Company, Inc.

www.xulonpress.com

DEDICATION

This assignment is dedicated to everyone who had to face some storms in their lives but have taken on the mind setting that they have been in the storm too long and if things are going to be different and better that the journey must first begin with them.

Words from the Author

In this walk of life, we will experience many uncertainties as well as setbacks and trying to figure out how to override them can make us feel as if we have just entered a maze.

The more we feel that we're heading toward the exit, the more we find ourselves right back where we began.

If we are not careful, it will appear as if we are slipping into a black hole and all hope appears hopeless. But the truth is even though we might not know one another, we all have experience some similar pains or the exact pain which have left many with more scars than one can count, but the good news is, if we share our experiences, it will provide hope to the next person that they can overcome in spite of what it looks like now.

I wrote this book out of many years of pain from family, friends and sadly to say, even religious folks, that I have helped down through the years who left a very bitter taste in my mouth, leaving me with the mind setting of having nothing to do with church, or the people who attend and far as some family and friends to me, cutting them off made sense.

The reality of all this was it was hurting me more than any of them. Why do I believe this? It is because they appear to be moving on with their lives in spite of all the deceitful things *they have done as if nothing has happened while looking at me or you as if we're the problem.*

As for me, it appeared as if I was living a double life. What I mean is in spite of what I was feeling, I was always there giving and doing all I could, at the same time feeling like I was being used and resenting every moment of it. What was even worse was I was teaching others concerning biblical beliefs and not really applying them to myself as a result of my disappointments like many of you.

Seeing me for what I had become was not good, neither was it righteous nor Godly because I read where God said, "I know your works: you are neither cold nor hot. Would that you were either cold or hot! So because you are lukewarm and neither hot nor cold, I will spit you out of my mouth." Reading this stopped me right in my tracks because I—who teaches on love, respect, and forgiveness—found myself coming up short. If I can see myself, how many others are like me who want to be set free from bitterness and disappointments but just don't know how? Disappointments have no respect of persons, but how one handles them can be messy. It's truly a journey to overcome life situations the awakening that follows is priceless.

I hope my sharing with you is just as enlightening for you as it was for me; enjoy the journey and new found freedom that I am confident that you will find.

ACKNOWLEDGMENT

I could have not completed this assignment without the support and encouragement from those who believed that I could make a difference in other people lives by constantly motivating me and giving me the strength to believe all things are possible if I just stay focused and have faith that I can do it.

PREFACE

**Forgiving Others Means Forgiving Yourself
In Your Journey Lies Your Awakening**

This book is written to help believers, nonbelievers and encourage everyone to face those giants that have been robbing them of their peace and wholeness. Giants that have left many with doubt and questions that appear to be challenging, hopeless and fearful as they wonder within their thoughts, "Will those grey clouds ever roll away and allow the sun to shine once again?"

Many times, we ask ourselves, "Is it possible for one to make sudden changes when our dreams and hopes have been tainted or shattered by circumstances beyond one's control?" Those giants of pain, hurt, guilt and despair including forgiving others from years of disappointing experiences have left many with the question of will they ever recover from such strong blows?

In life, many individuals will face some form of regret, shame, embarrassment as well as denial and recovery from such bad experiences is not always an easy task to overcome.

Challenges can take away one's strength and ability, leaving them broken, full of hurt as despair sets in and depression takes over. The truth of the matter is to never allow someone to be your priority while allowing yourself to be your option, but face those giants and seek help by enquiring and asking questions like, "What is the solution when you have lost trust and fear has crept in?"

When individuals have dedicated themselves with loyalty, how do you suddenly make change when your dreams and hopes have been tainted by no fault of your own? How do you bounce back after your world has been broken into many pieces like shattered glass? Where do you go when the place you used to attend for refuge is no longer a safe haven? After years of dedicated service, out of nowhere the rug is pulled from under you without warning.

How can one find faith in God when church members and leaders have led them astray? With so much hurt and pain, is it possible for such a one to be revived again? What steps can be made in order for one to let go and let God again?

These are statements that people make on a day to day basis after being led down the wrong path by someone that they loved and trusted. From time to time, many people will find themselves in a rut, dreading whether or not their today will be better than their yesterday.

In life, many are trying to rebuild from past hurts encountered by maybe one's spouse, parents, children, preacher, teacher, or even a close friend. But whatever the situation is, these are situations that have caused many people hurt and pain that will eventually cause resentment as non-forgiveness enters the equation.

Maybe you have experienced some of these situations and if so, this book is for you or a loved one who is ready to recover and move into their destiny.

Just in case you have been blessed to not have encountered these issues but you know someone who has, I recommend you encourage them to read this book because in return, they will thank you for being a part of their recovery because many have not prepared or possess the necessary tools for successfully and effectively weathering the disappointments that life will sometimes bring.

TABLE OF CONTENTS

Introduction xiii

Chapter 1	Thoughts of Uncertainty	17
Chapter 2	Identity	26
Chapter 3	Life Lessons	35
Chapter 4	Your Words Control Your Results	41
Chapter 5	Visiting the Person Within	46
Chapter 6	How to Stop the Hurting	61
Chapter 7	Remove the Toxins	77
Chapter 8	After the Storm Is Over	89
Chapter 9	Getting Pass the Roadblocks	97
Chapter 10	Don't Count Me Out	110
Chapter 11	Remove the Mask; It's Morning	117

About the Author 129
Very Special Thanks 131
Contact the Author 133

Introduction

Many people are suffering from much despair and hurt that is beyond their control. They have become very fragile and crippled by that thing called fear. They constantly appear to be in the now when being spoken to, but at the same time, you will notice them drifting as if they have taken a trip, staring into space and not once really hearing a word that has been spoken to them. It's apparent that overwhelming situations have crept in, leaving them in an uncertain place of doubt and unbelief, feeling insecure in the things they once believed in. They are second guessing themselves when it pertains to their relationships and belief in their God.

There was a time when the preacher would say just trust in God and everything would be alright. But the question today is how can one believe or trust what the minister is saying when the divorce rate in the church world is more than forty five percent and church leaders are divorcing like national holidays? While others are constantly on a day to day basis faced with one crisis or another, the thoughts of throwing in the towel make sense.

Someone once asked this question: "Have you ever had someone interrupt your life? Or made you feel like you are the one who is out of control and you are the reason why they behave the way they do? Leaving one questioning, how in the hell did things escalated from zero to ten; why you didn't hear the countdown? But yet at the same time, trying to figure out what is real, and why did they allow someone to pull them into behaviors that are unimaginable and unbelievable. For many have experience such situations and have survived, but not without some form of scars closely related to bitterness and resentment.

Many have made statements that they can forgive a person who has apologized and asked for forgiveness, but the question of doubt still lingers in the back of their mind concerning the sincerity of the individual's apology.

Experienced pain which include deception and deceitfulness has taken a grip on many, leaving them with doubt as they began to believe that nothing seems to be sincere even when one wants to believe. And as a result of this, one will constantly find themselves being faced with insecurities as fear surfaces from being stung on numerous occasion.

Someone once said that forgiveness is a funny thing; it warms the heart and cools the sting. In other words, once a person comes to the reality of releasing what was done to them, now they can truly move on and feel serenity because the thoughts of what was done to them no longer carries that weight of uncertainty but brings about calmness like a pinch that only lasted for a moment.

I read a prayer once that said to forgive like thee, blessed son of God! Take this as the law of my life. You have given the command and have placed great power within us. You have loved us enough to forgive us and will also fill us with love and teach us to forgive others.

Replies have been made that forgiveness is hard to extend because it demands that people let go of something that they value which is not a piece of jewelry but pride. Contrary to what might be expected, one can look back on experiences that seem especially desolating and painful and be a help to others.

A man by the name of General Oglethrope once commended to John Wesley that he will never forgive and

Introduction

never forget and John Wesley response back to him was, "Sir I hope you never sin." I believe that Mr. Wesley understood that in life we as a people don't always get it right, but the time will come when we will need someone to be understanding with us when we fall short because the truth is everyone will fall short in one thing or another. But how one regroups will determine the difference in their survival.

I was enlightened by a statement I once heard that said quitters never win and winners never quit. And as I began to meditate on that statement, I began to understand what the individual was saying. If you make up your mind that you can't forgive even when you haven't tried, how do you know if you can? I don't agree with the statement just get over it, but I will say that if you work toward it, you will eventually get over it. Why? Because holding on to what someone said or did is not helping but it is hurting and hindering many from great potential.

An elderly woman once commended that she had a very bad marriage and became very bitter and angry toward her husband and meddling in laws. She said that he had children outside of the marriage and was very abusive to her and her children. As a result of this abuse, she began seeking help from those she believed could help her only to experience negative remarks and comments that were unbelievable.

Those she went to for help told her that he was her husband so just deal with it because she wouldn't be able to find another man who would want her with all those children. She tried to no avail as things went from one extreme to the next. Her abuse became more and more intolerable, causing her to do what was unbelievable to many that knew her. She left not knowing where she was going or what she was going to do. It was told to her that she would be back because she would never make it on her own.

Many times in this woman's life, things seemed so uncertain. The struggles at times were more than she thought she could endure as the thoughts of returning kept entering in her mind on several occasions. But as she pondered those thoughts, her mind reflected on the devastation her children experienced, and she found the strength to keep it moving.

With little education and no real job training, her struggle became very hard as rage begin to set in. She had to do the unthinkable and apply for food stamps and welfare while trying hard not to allow her mind to be tormented by the negative remarks that were spoken to her concerning her dreams and happiness. But because of her iron will, she realized that if she didn't find a purpose for her life, her children's future as well as her own future was heading toward a dead end road.

She began to realize that if she wanted to make a change, she had to find her destiny and the only way she could find it would be through her recovery.

She began to make statements like, "I'm going to put my husband in God's hands and focus on these children." And as a result of not allowing herself to continue to drown in her misfortune, she learned how to balance a check book, went to night school, got a degree and became very successful.

But just imagine if she would have allowed herself to stay in that rut. What would have been her outcome? But her attitude was "if it's meant to be, it is up to me in spite of broken promises and disappointments." This woman illustrated that just because a thing is broken and damaged does not mean that it is not repairable.

In life, there will be disappointments, but don't quit! Take on the attitude that I heard someone say which was quitters never win and winners never quit because broken dreams and broken promises unfortunately are a part of life, but how one handles it after a period of time will determine the outcome of it.

Chapter One

THOUGHTS OF UNCERTAINTY

While preparing to be one of the spokespersons at a church conference, I couldn't seem to focus; my mind just couldn't seem to settle on one thing. I seemed to be going in many directions and right when I thought I had something, I became unsatisfied and agitated.

I just couldn't seem to pull anything together as frustration began to get the upper hand and to make matters worse, time was slipping away, way too fast because I was having a Murphy's Law type of day that truly appeared that everything was going wrong. If I could have turned the hands of time back, I would have, but that was wishful thinking as things began to go from one extreme to the next.

Fortunately for me, my husband reminded me of some past materials that he thought would do and suggested that I consider revisiting those materials because I might just find what I needed.

I believed it to be a great ideal at the time, but I still wasn't satisfied. Nothing was clicking and it was getting closer to the time of the event, and still I found myself with nothing. I came to the conclusion that behaving like a two year old because things just aren't going my way made matters worse.

I had to get a grip, pull it together, and get some prospective because this behavior was not working.

Quietly calming myself, I began to ask my Heavenly Father to give me what to present because by this time, I wasn't feeling it, but the clock was still ticking.

As I began to calm my nerves and review some previous materials, I ran across a paper dealing with people who are unable to forgive. It was as if a light was turned on and I started saying to myself, "I got it. I want to speak on unresolved hurts that are hindering many people."

Then, all of a sudden, for no apparent reason, I began second guessing myself and making all types of excuses as I began to find fault within myself on why it wouldn't work. Now, as a result of my uncertainties, I was second guessing myself and justifying myself with one excuse or another just in case things didn't turn out the way I thought they should.

The clock was ticking and I had less than thirty minutes before the seminar was to begin, and I couldn't seem to shake or remove the thoughts that were going on within me. Those thoughts of uncertainties entrap most people and hinder their potential of stepping out and reaching their goals and dreams that lie within them.

I began to say within myself that I could do this and I would do this because if not, I will be like those that become trapped and have regret from second guessing themselves and questioning themselves on how things would have turned out, if they would have just made an attempt to give it a chance. So, I began to meditate quietly within as I asked my Heavenly Father to give me what to say concerning forgiveness and to my surprise, it was received very well.

I found myself in an overwhelmed place as I thanked God for his guidance because I wasn't sure how this was going to turn out at the last minute.

Realizing that it pays not to follow that old saying of don't put off tomorrow what you can do today became very enlightening as I found myself becoming speechless by many of the comments.

Listening to how many people were saying when others would try to tell them about certain things that they couldn't hear, but how someone else comes along with the exact message and present it in a different way, is eye opening.

It reminded me of a conversation I heard that said, if a person cooks a beautiful meal and place it on a lovely tray and serves it, that a person would dined from it, but you take that same dish and place it on a trash can lid and try to serve it, and the results would be different. Why? Because how one presents a thing will determine how it's received.

It's sort of like those thoughts of uncertainties that will interrupt a person's thinking pattern, throwing them completely off course, as the things they need to do won't get done and the consequences that follow will be sloppy, revealing behaviors that will produce results leaving many with nothing left but doubt and unbelief, wondering if they will ever discover true fulfillment.

Humbled by what I was hearing, especially when they begin to say, for years they had been carrying certain things from their past that they thought they would never release. But after hearing and seeing themselves, it gave them an opportunity to reconsider because some hadn't spoken to relatives since they were in their teens and now have families of their own.

There were so many questions and all I could say to myself was, "What if I allowed my uncertainties to hinder me from following through because I lacked confidence within myself?" But after that morning seminar and a couple of days later, for some reason I couldn't seem to get that lesson out of my mind.

The Journey

Everywhere that I went and lectured I found myself teaching on forgiveness. It was as if I was being drawn to dig deeper into this subject. Why? At the time, I didn't understand it, but as I began my search, things began to become clearer to me.

My quest began within the religious community in order to get the best clarity possible. As I listened to many of them, I realized that people of faith whose convictions are second to none who claimed to be believers have a problem with forgiving. They have been carrying pounds of unresolved disappointments with them for many years—things that a past preacher or deacon said as well as hurts from church mothers and ushers.

So many people of faith are silently still hurting and hovering over things that happened many years ago while deliberately refusing to release it or just don't know how or who to talk to for help. Some of them believe that it is okay to hold on to what someone did to them because their opinion is that person is going to get just what they deserve. This disturbed me because this should not be named among people who say they believe in a forgiving God but won't allow themselves to forgive.

Continuing my quest, I stumbled over information implying that some leaders are worse than some of the people that they serve. Flabbergasted by what I was discovering, it left me wondering, speechless, and questioning those things that were being said. How did they arrive at that place of uncertainty? As I begin to look deeper into the matter, I begin to understand their experience of pain down through the years.

Their pain from years of hard work, dedication, as well as sacrifice and disappointments in a people that they invested in only to be betrayed left them with a bitter taste as well as a lack of confidence and trust in those around them. They have the attitude of what goes around comes around and what many of them say to others concerning forgiveness they really don't apply to themselves.

Many will admit that they really need help in this particular area because they not only need to release their pain, but they want to let go of the past and move on. Some even believe that they will be lost if they don't repent from this, but they have become like the child who got mad at their friends and took their marbles and went home angry with an attitude of "who needs them anyway."

Some will even say that maybe they have overreacted and need to let it go, but that thing called pride has set in. They prefer to sit back and hide behind that ole saying of, "the Lord will fight their battle and bring those who they believed wronged them to their senses rather than ask for forgiveness."

As I continued to try to digest some of the information that I was gathering, I couldn't help but wonder if they ever heard that saying "do unto to others as you would have them to do unto you." But until one can truly see themselves, they wait until the other person confronts them first, because by doing this, it would be easier to say to the other person that they are sorry too.

But is this a good place for a believer to be? Because I read somewhere that pride is an inordinate opinion of one's own dignity. One must realize that it is important to keep in mind that pride takes the focus off of our values and the end results are never good, because if one is not careful, that thing called pride will make one's image more than one's reality.

A proud person will easily fall into that trap of serving themselves instead of serving their God, which will become dangerous as one begins to develop disdainful behaviors while disregarding the Proverb that declare that when pride comes and then comes dishonor.

Many would argue and say this is understandable, but I still wondered within my thoughts, "What if people that they had wronged in their life never gave them another opportunity and regarded them as unworthy of a second chance?" Realistically, some have not only been given a second chance, but many opportunities to get things right and move on with their lives for the better.

But most importantly, what if the God that they say they truly believe in had not forgiven them of their shortcomings? You see, the truth of the matter is, we don't always, as human beings, get it right. We slip and fall sometimes, say and do things out of character and the wrong people are affected by our behavior. Often times, when we realize how our negative actions have wounded the innocent, we will find ourselves hoping that things work out in our favor after we have done something out of the ordinary.

While continuing to meditate concerning this matter, I thought within myself that maybe because the majority of leaders strive to do what is right, they have this notion or impression that everyone should respect and accept them for the good deeds they have done toward others and their families. But since this is not always the case, most of them will find themselves in a slum.

Not realizing nor understanding at the time the severity of their pain will lead them slowly slipping into a deep depression as anguish sets in by over powering them, leaving them distracted from the assignment in which they say they were called to do.

Puzzled by let downs and hurts from people who unfortunately have left them with some serious scares will find themselves questioning their calling as they begin to fade away in their night season, walking away from the thing that they cherish and love the most, feeling like a total failure.

It's like that business partner who invested everything just to be deceived, found themselves questioning whether or not they have what it takes to continue the path that they once believed in.

As I continued to try to understand this issue, I began to realize that the reason why the majority of people struggle so much is because, even though they "try hard" to make the change, they are actually trying to force the change from the outside. But the truth of the matter is that we should start on the inside and let the change work its way out.

One must keep in mind that true forgiveness is mostly for one's piece of mind, health and with those who play a very important part in our lives. For it has been stated that learning to forgive definitely requires God's grace because without it, people will continue to feel that if they haven't wronged someone, why do they need to be the one to say "I am sorry" or be the one to let it go?

Truthfulness

Forgiveness always seems to be so easy when we need it and so hard when we need to give it. Forgiveness forces one to grow beyond what or who you think you are. It rolls your burdens away and sets us free and enlarges our future, but most importantly, forgiveness tastes sweet. Many will hesitate and say this makes sense, but the truth of the matter is when someone does us wrong, we don't always confront the individual, but we will begin talking to other people about how upset we are and how deceitful we believe the other party is.

Constantly telling others about the problems and not realizing that the words of a talebearer are wounds, they go down into the innermost parts of the belly which bring about negative responses from others as the conversation go from one extreme to the next, allowing an entrance for people who are unfamiliar with the issue to say things that they shouldn't say, and now other people who only know one side of the story is feeling empathy for them.

Opinions are developed toward someone that they have maybe the half truth about and not the whole truth because the other person is not there to defend themselves. Now, we have a situation where individuals are destroying someone's character by what someone said instead of what they really know. As a result of this gossip, they become so quick to pass judgment as they find themselves in the middle of a mess, not knowing how they arrived there.

Now when the truth comes out, the blame game begins as a result of what he said, she said and they said.

Instead of listening, many will comment on what one has heard because gossip always appears to be so juicy that many fail to realize the harm that they are inflicting on others as a result of what they heard instead of what they know.

Putting the cart before the horse can be damaging to those who become the victim as a result of another's wounds. How easier things would be if many would just develop the mind setting that when someone is degrading others as a result of their pain; remind them that they need to come to grips with themselves because they are out of control. But instead, many will believe what has been said and develop a negative opinion instead of questioning the person's intentions who brought about this gossip in the first place.

Maybe opinions would be different if many would apply that passage that says, "Which one of you that is without a fault cast the first stone." But instead, many will become a member of that club called confusion because the person who is being accused might not have said anything. Consequently, this is how people get into trouble because it's pure hear say. So as you can see, we become like the person who is bringing the gossip because we never confronted the accuser. We have so much to say concerning a matter that we really know nothing about.

Now when the accuser finds out what is being said concerning them and they try to explain what they did say, we develop an attitude because something in us or a gut feeling is telling us that we have reacted too soon.

So I say again, why should we ask for forgiveness? Just take a moment and think about it. Who is really at fault here? Especially if one says they are sorry if they said anything to hurt or offend. Or have we gotten to a point within ourselves that we are so perfect and righteous that every choice or decision that we make is right?

If that be the case, ask yourself, how did you responded to that person who touched a nerve at a teacher's parent conference. What about the waiter at the restaurant, the cashier, better yet, what was your speech when the car in front of you cut you off with no signals?

Can we keep it real, people? Did we give them that finger that is not the index finger? Did we give them a few choice words like? Well! You know what I 'm thinking, or did we just smile and say have a good day or God bless you?

We must keep in mind that behind closed doors those who live with us really knows us and how often have they forgiven us?

We have gone from one extreme to the next, whether it was mismanaging money, screaming and yelling at the children, a little slip of the lip and on occasion, that little white lie that was spoken so easily without any hesitation when we didn't want to deal with the consequences after making a mess of things.

One let down to another, but for the most part, spouses forgave, our children didn't stop loving us, and our Heavenly Father never gave up on us. So every time we find ourselves in a place that we believe that we can't forgive or we refuse to forgive, be true to thy self by remembering when you didn't have it all together loved ones and friends found a way in their hearts to forgive you.

Chapter Two

IDENTITY

It has been said that identity gives one information concerning whom they are, the way you think concerning yourself, the way you are viewed by the world and the characteristics that define you. Identity provides us with the means of answering the question "who am I?"

Many people choose to believe that their character and personality are one of the same, but the truth is one's character refers to the morals that a person has and their penchants to do the right things. Personality deals with the images that one projects how other people perceive them and how they deal with other people. Personality is on the surface, but character is deep inside and one can almost fake their personality. But they can't fake their character because our character is who we really are and our personality is what we seem to be.

We that say we believe in a higher power or have faith-like beliefs should be very mindful that we don't appear to be so over the edge with our beliefs that we put blinders on and miss what our Heavenly Father is trying to reveal unto us.

We have to make sure that we are not sending out the wrong signals that we think is our character, but the truth is it's our personality because we have no idea who is taking notes concerning us.

Identity

When was the last time we really questioned ourselves when it pertained to our conduct or realness to our everyday beliefs? Are we showing forth the love we talk about? Or are we like a balloon that's full of air that's about to explode?

While continuing to show our true identity, we must keep in mind that we can't be behaving differently than our speech because our true colors will begin to surface.

But oh what webs we continue to reed when one thinks that they are all that with some chips along with something to sip while living in their glass houses, throwing stones at others while failing to see the cracks in their own lives.

Many have become like those cracks on a windshield when left alone; it will continue to spread, but if the right pothole is hit, that glass will spatter. But until then, one will continue to ride on those tracks from one part of town to another pulling their cargo of bitterness to everyone that will listen while continuing to give them a cover story which is theirs.

We make statements like, "You can't trust a word that they say because they don't mean what they say." "You don't know them like I do" and "Don't let them fool you by that so called sincere talk of being regretful because it is just an act and I'll never forgive them because they say they are sorry."

Some even go to the degree of saying they would rather die than forgive. What a harsh way of thinking. It reminds me of the man in the bible who wanted mercy from the bill collector, but when it was time for him to show mercy, he forgot. I heard someone say that the same God who forgives us is the same God who is going to judge us.

Now, I'll be the first one to say at times in my life, it was hard to forgive certain people that I helped get through there storms who forgot all about me when things improved in their lives. Or the time I believed in someone who others had spoken very negative of and when things improved for them, they walked past me and didn't speak to me as if I was dirt under their shoe or even worse.

I know that people can hurt you so, but if we would apply the statement that we quote concerning being more than a conquer, we wouldn't act the way we do but instead become the bigger person and allow it to be an experience that we can learn from and teach others that might be experiencing something similar.

But instead, many will stick with that old saying that to change a person of their will, they are of the same opinion still as they continue to add more fuel to the flame.

I'm reminded of the statement that King David made that said when he is overwhelmed, he could ask his God to take him to a rock that is greater than him. David not only believed but he knew that his God could take the hurt away.

If we refuse to trust in what our closest friends are saying and don't have confidence in the God that we claim to believe in like David, we will find ourselves in the same situation. What if our God took on the same mind setting as we have when we ask him to forgive us and he says no way, you're too far gone! What then?

I know that would be a serious problem for most of us because the first thing one would say they thought God was a God of love and that he is, but like parents who love their children, they must correct them when they are wrong. Because if they don't, they will think that their behavior is acceptable only to find out that down the road their actions can be costly as well as devastating.

Not long ago, I was having a conversation with a family member concerning some family issues and to my surprise they began to explain to me that the problem in the family was this:

One brother had a problem with another brother. The brothers began to create problems throughout the family, not realizing the damage that they were creating.

Now you have children upset with certain uncles, aunts and cousin about a situation they really know nothing about.

Identity

As a result of their fathers, they were never invited to family gatherings, only to be treated as second class citizens and strangers. But what was more astonishing was no one could recall what the disagreement or confrontation was all about.

I recall reading in the bible about Abram's wife Sarai who couldn't bare her husband any children that she desperately wanted and as I continued to read about Sarai, it was stated that she asked her husband to lay with her handmaid Hagar so that she can have a child or as we would say in today's time, be a surrogates.

Unfortunately, Sarah didn't consider the consequences that would follow like many who seek surrogates will find themselves having some resentment issues as they watch the other individuals carry what they wish they could have done themselves, even though they agreed to it.

Sadly to say, some surrogates find themselves in a situation as well because they failed to count up the cost as they pondered in their heart whether or not they can just walk away from something that has become a part of them for months.

Sarah's emotions toward her handmaid went from one extreme to another as envy began to set in as it became apparent that she was not handling the situation well. Sarah was spiraling out of control as those around her begin to feel the effects of her wrath from a plan not well thought out or a plan that just went bad.

Now, because of Sarah's rage and jealous behavior, you have two brothers caught in the middle of a situation that not only had nothing to do with them, it didn't even concern them, but yet they are experiencing the hostility and animosity from it.

One can only imagine how uncomfortable it was for the two brothers at times as they watched and listened to their mother's bickering.

Two brothers who loved one another at times found themselves in an uncomfortable situation as well as in a mess that had nothing to do with them. As the result of a plan gone bad they continued to find themselves caught in the middle of someone else's drama and that is exactly what happens, when innocent people are pulled in other people's issues.

I've heard stories about how families can live in the same town and never visit one another over things like one thought they were better than the other when one would say they worked hard while the other did nothing but sit around criticizing and complaining and now expects the family to do everything for them.

Some years ago, my personality and character was put on display and I had to make sure that I didn't allow myself to be a part of issues concerning certain family members. Truthfully speaking, it was difficult to say the least.

My father had just passed away and certain family members from his side of the family for no apparent reason never reached out to his children and to make matters worse, in my opinion, they wouldn't even break bread with us.

I couldn't believe nor understand their behavior, especially when we were never disrespectful to them or anything like that because our mother didn't raise us like that and our dad would not have allowed such behavior, so I had to let it go.

After the repast, I begin meditating on the chain of events that had taken place and was proud of how well my brothers and sisters conducted themselves in spite of what didn't happen.

I began to say to myself, "Daddy (Fats) would have been proud of us." But if any of us would have made a scene, we would have been acting like the two brothers I mentioned earlier. That cycle would have started all over again, making us no better than them.

As a result of not being able to sleep due to the chain of events that were encountered earlier during that day, I became moved by watching a television special concerning a man who was a successful song writer as well as a great movie producer.

I found myself surprised as I listened to the host make comments on how depressed and angry this man was. It was stated that this man was a successor for forty years and that many artist would envy him today because most don't last ten years.

Trying to understand how this man succumbed and allowed anguish to put him in a place of insecurity making him so bitter was unbelievable. Continuing to hear all his associates make statements that they believed that he died from a broken heart, filled with much despair, never recovering from his disappointments was a wow moment.

What a tragedy and misfortune that such a great man, so ahead of his time, would allow such past hurts and disappointments to overpower him.

My thoughts were with all of this success; one would look back over their lives and enjoy the fruit of their labor, but he never recovered from past hurts by them that he trusted and invested in.

Is it possible that we look for acceptance from others because of something we lack within ourselves? We allow other's opinions to determine our success or failures instead of appreciating the gift's that lies within us.

I remember hearing a conversation concerning a minister who was a great teacher at his church and well respected by many, but he had a problem forgiving his fifteen year old daughter. It was said that he forbid his daughter from seeing this young man and his daughter disobeyed him and became pregnant.

He felt so betrayed by his daughter that he put her out of the home and wanted nothing to do with her as a result of feeling nothing but disrespect, embarrassment and shame that he believed she brought to the family. His concern was whether the congregation would still want him as their leader.

Better yet, what would they think of him instead of seeing that his daughter needed him?

As a result of his disappointment, he became so enraged that he forgot that his teachings on compassion didn't only apply to those that he taught, but to his daughter as well. In his rage, he forgot that teenagers don't always make right decisions and if the truth be told, neither did he.

Being blindsided by the reactions he thought that he would receive from the congregation wouldn't allow him to see that if he would have just showed his daughter some compassion. Just maybe it would help her from the negative choices that she would continue to make. He failed to realize that his rejection of her would have her looking for love in all the wrong places and wrong faces.

But like most people, he forgot that someone in his life showed compassion toward him when he needed it the most even though he might not have deserved it.

I can only imagine the disappointment felt by the father who had the prodigal son in the bible. This son no longer wanted to be under his father's authority and wanted to do whatever he wanted to do. This son did many things against the morals and principals that he was taught. It was stated that this prodigal son was wasting his money, drinking and just out of control.

But what truly intrigued me the most concerning this story was how the father handled the whole situation, especially believing that his son would do the right thing, but instead he chose to do the opposite.

Just like many children today who have left their parent's home, the parents expect them to do the right thing. Unfortunately discovering that they have gone buck wild, leaving parents puzzled and wondering what the heck has happened to that child because who they have become is not how they were raised.

When things got worse as a result of how the prodigal son mismanaged his inheritance or as we would say in today's time, that when he spent everything on his wants instead of taking care of his needs—he found himself in an unfamiliar place that had him compromising his standards and taking a job that was against his Jewish upbringings.

Feeding swine to a Jewish person in biblical times was unbearably degrading because the keeping and feeding swine was forbidden. What I admired about this whole story was this: when the son realized that he done wrong and messed up, he went back to his father, making no excuses but took responsibility while asking for his father's help.

Most importantly, the father chose to show forth not only love toward his son but forgiveness by receiving him with open arms without being concerned about what other people might have thought or said.

It has been said that Jewish men in biblical times held on to their integrity no matter what without compromise, but this father not only showed his true character, but had the spirit of our Heavenly Father because when we do wrong or have done wrong and we ask him to forgive us, he does.

Maybe if many of us keep the story of the prodigal son before us we would make better decisions when it concerns our love ones and friends who disappoint us.

I believe that, if the believer would just remember how they were forgiven in time past when they didn't deserve it, they would find themselves relieved with unbelief when mercy was shown unto them. In spite of all of their faults, they were given another chance.

If only one could only remember that in time past that they didn't always get it right, that their lives could be a help to many with their testimonies of how they overcame situations that seem impossible. Maybe they can come to the realization that yesterday's issues only matters when one continues to let it take root, but once spring cleaning takes place, those dark clouds that use to hang over dissipates as if the issues never existed.

But until then, we have a responsibility to continue praying for them because all of us have or had an issue with one thing or another, but God never gave up on us.

Chapter Three

LIFE LESSONS

$\mathcal{M}$any people have gone through such things that could have destroyed them. The hurt, pain and criticism could have made them bitter and unforgiving, but instead they took lemons and made lemonade.

I can recall the time hearing my father make a statement that when I was born, all his problems started, or the time when my favorite uncle was dying and needed to confess to me the real reason why he always had a special place in his heart for me.

I remembered taking a deep breath as I sat on the couch next to him as the palms of my hands began to sweat from nervousness. Why did I all of a sudden become nervous? I didn't know, but what I did know was that whatever it was, it had been disturbing him, too. He began by asking me questions like if I could recall the times that he would say to me that this was my home and that I was always welcomed there at any time.

The more he began to ask me questions concerning my childhood, the more uneasy I became. He began to explain to me that when I was born, I was given to him, for how long, I can't recall because I was stung with unbelief by what I was hearing.

"In Your Journey Lies Your Awakening"

At first I thought he was hallucinating and getting me mixed up with someone else due to his failing health. But as I continued to listen to him express how he felt when I was ripped from his arms, reality clicked in and all doubt was removed. I knew he was not hallucinating. He began to inform me that I had a right to know because everyone else not only knew about this deep dark secret that had been hidden from me, but it was the talk at every family gathering and every kitchen table.

You talk about hitting below the belt, that announcement was enough to make anyone's knees buckle as all sorts of thoughts begin to race through my mind. All I kept saying to myself was, "what the duh?" My thoughts begin to get the better part of me as I continued to sit beside him with nothing but blankness on my face.

Fighting back tears and becoming angry with him for not telling me sooner was a bit much. So many mixed emotions consumed me with questions and things I wanted to say but I didn't know how, but yet at the same time, I believed the reason why he didn't tell me was because he was trying to protect me, which made it worse.

Watching his frail body and facing the reality that one of the most important people in my life would soon be departing with no returning back was enough to deal with to say the least.

Finding strength and staying in the moment while realizing that he was dying and knowing that confession is good for the soul kept me from storming out and asking all sorts of questions. I realized in that moment that family secrets can stir up a war that will not only affect the guilty, but can ruin the lives of the innocent as well.

After realizing that burden that he had been carrying around for years and all the time that was wasted with deception and guilt that was a thorn to him for many years, I decided to swallow my anger and stay in the moment because enough time had been wasted with secrets and shame and I did not want my last memories with my favorite uncle to be one of regrets.

As I begin to grasp to this best kept family secret that everyone knew except for me, I began to understand why I was treated differently, teased and not fully accepted by certain family members.

The more I tried to understand the matter, the more upset and angry I became. I refused to attend his funeral because I felt like the first person who said anything to me I would completely lose it and let them have it. Instead of embarrassing myself, I felt like running away without looking back from a undeserving group of people, but I couldn't do that either because I kept thinking where or who would I run to. When those who claim to love me don't want me, who will accept me?

You talk about mind boggling that was one. Now, unfortunately I had to deal with that nagging war of confusion that was going on in my mind. That war of rejection, neglect and deception began to win the battle in my mind and over my life with a stronghold. Sadly to say, during that period of my life, my relationship at that time with my Heavenly Father wasn't in good standards because I had allowed negative experiences from certain individuals of faith to cloud my view, so prayer for me was not one of my options.

As a result of my competiveness, I looked at this unfortunate situation as a challenge that had my back up against the wall and it was decision making time. I had to see the glass that I was looking through being either half empty with no hope or half full with many possibilities. As painful as this was for me, I had to accept the fact that this battle that I was dealing with belonged to someone else and that I just happen to be in the mix of it by no choice of my own.

After much agonizing and self- pity that I put on myself as a result of someone else's guilt who was only thinking about themselves and not the pain that they had caused me, I had to come to the conclusion that this was a losing battle and enough damage had already been done.

I had to make a decision and come to grips that my life was not defined by what one thinks of me or how one sees me, but it is defined and designed by how I see me.

During this process of accepting this reality, I began to learn that our lives are not determined by what happens to us, but how we react to what happens to us. It is not by what life brings to us that controls us, but it is by the attitude we bring to life. This experience taught me that a positive or negative attitude causes a chain reaction to whatever the outcome might be.

There are many that have gone through some devastating experiences in their lives, but they have found an inner strength to forgive and move on when others would say they have a right to remain bitter and angry about what happened to them, but they chose not to be a victim but to be victorious.

Those before us showed that we don't have to hold on to bitterness but take the bitter and turn it into something great.

Thomas Edison who we see as a success now failed, according to reports, thousands of times before he could get an electric bulb to work. How embarrassing this could have been, but giving up was not one of his options in spite of all the negative rumors that had been said concerning him. Yet he continued to work without ceasing until he got the desired results that he was looking for.

How embarrassing this would have been for many, but his focus was on the idea that if he'd continually work at it, he would get the desired results that he was looking for and change the mind setting of many who gave up on him. Because while many had so much to say, he knew within that he had what it took to make it happen.

At times, many accused him of being unreasonable and difficult to deal with. But I would say that Mr. Edison was focused on his destiny and giving up was not an option as he set the bar high, taking away all excuses. And as a result of it, we can thank Mr. Edison every time we hit the switch and on comes the lights.

It was stated that Abraham Lincoln couldn't win at anything. He lost his girlfriend who was the love of his life, failed in business, defeated not only in the race for Illinois House Speaker but nomination for Congress as well just to name a few. And to add insult to injury, he had a nervous breakdown. One would think surely it's time to run and hide under a rock away from it all, but instead he never gave up and became one of the greatest presidents in 1861 in the United States of America.

In the year of 1947, history was made when an American woman by the name of Edith Ronnie was the first woman to set foot on the Antarctica continent and was the first woman in the world to be a working member of an Antarctica expedition. Just image the odds against her especially during those days and the backlash that her husband received for supporting her. And as a result of it, she became the first non-royal woman to have an Antarctic site named after her because of staying focused when the odds were against her.

One can only imagine all the crazy rumors that were surrounding the oval office in 1981 when President Ronald Regan appointed Sandra Day O' Connor as the first female of the Supreme Court of the United States. The things that she had to endure as well, but because of her endurance she was regarded as the court's leading centrist and was the swing vote in many cases which made her the most powerful justice for many years and as the result of this, doors have been opened to others.

There are so many life lessons that we can learn from others who, in spite of their struggles, made it because their destiny was based on how well they responded to the negativity that was presented to them and because of it, showed us that nothing is impossible.

Just image all the people that were told that they would never succeed because of where they came from, or who their parents were, or lack of education, or because of their disabilities, but yet they still succeeded.

There are so many people that we can learn from who had oppositions, but they didn't remain bitter; they triumphed through it all.

Those who came before us, in spite of their challenges, left a legacy for those who were coming behind them as a result of staying focused as they kept it moving. But most importantly, they did not hold a grudge because they believed in themselves.

> **So** *what are you allowing to be a thorn in your life that's hindering you from stepping out and becoming the person you believe you can be if you could only find the strength to rise above it?*

Chapter Four

YOUR WORDS CONTROL YOUR RESULTS

The proverb tells us that the tongue that brings healing is a tree of life, but a deceitful tongue crushes the spirit. It had been said that the real art of a conversation is not only to say the right things at the right time, but to leave unsaid the wrong thing at the tempting time.

When we are not careful with our words, we involve other people who now have an opinion about something they really know nothing about. The sad thing about this situation is that the cycle doesn't end.

What is even worse is we can't see that instead of demonstrating or showing someone the values we proclaim to process, we send out signals that echo like thunder as we partake in the conversation by declaring we know exactly how the person is feeling by letting them know that they don't blame them at all because they would feel the same way too if it were them.

I read a passage that said to see to it that no one misses the grace of God and that no bitter root grows up to create trouble and defile many. In other words, we shouldn't be in the middle of conflict or hear say that causes a person to react in a way that brings nothing but negativity.

For instance take a person who doesn't have faith or really doesn't believe in God like most people, but they have such an inner strength within that helps them and believe that nothing is impossible while blocking out all negative remarks that were made concerning them and made it happen.

Have we, when we are so out done with others over a situation that happen many years ago, ever considered that maybe what happened was for the good and it's a blessing to realize it now because it could have been worse if you found out later?

I've heard many say the best thing that happen to them is when that person who they were so crazy about left them for someone else because the drama that the other person is going through could have been them.

If you ever take time to read about David and Saul in the bible, you will find out that for no apparent reason at all Saul wanted to kill David. You see, David was loyal to Saul, but that thing called jealousy overshadowed his judgment so badly that Saul sought out to not only destroy David, but to kill him.

But what I admired about David was he never said anything bad about Saul even though he didn't understand why Saul would want him dead, but Saul on the other hand turned people against David and made it very hard for him.

This is the same thing that some people do when they have issues with others; they say things that get other people involved as wrong opinions are developed. But David showed the true meaning of dignity and integrity while still having faith in his God, but what example are we showing? The scripture says that David behaved himself wisely in all his ways and that his Lord was with him.

Knowing that you have issues with forgiving people who you think wronged you as well as disappointed you, what results are you receiving from the things that you are saying and doing?

You know when people have unresolved issues it hinders their potential for becoming happy in life even when they succeed. What I mean is, if something happens to a person in 1969 and now it is 2009 and they are still angry concerning the matter especially when the other party has moved on, to me that person is still stuck in the time even though time is not standing still.

Just listen to their conversation when they speak concerning the matter; if you are not aware when the incident took place, you would think that it just happened and when you find out it was many years ago, you become puzzled with unbelief.

You see, unresolved issues causes problems in relationships. For example: A woman could have had a bad experience with a young man who she felt was the one until he deceived her and let her down. Now as a result of her disappointment with this individual, she began to label all men the same.

The truth of the matter is that there are some good men out there, because of her bad experience, she can't recognize one if he stood in front of her. He can be a hard worker, love her and respect her. But because she's still stuck in the past, she will chase him away not because he is no good but because she has unresolved issues.

Similar to a man who has had a bad experience with a woman, he will put all women in the same boat and will take on the mindset that you can't trust a woman and will miss the best thing that could happen to him.

You know sometimes people forget that they have done wrong things in their lives, just like the crowd who brought the woman to Jesus who was caught in adultery. I liked the way Jesus handled the situation by saying to them, "Which one of you that doesn't have a fault cast the first stone."

In other words, he made them take a look at themselves and that is what we should do when we have problems with people and we hold on to unnecessary things that pile up like junk that needs to be disposed of.

Written or spoken words are continuously propelling us through our day to day living as many find themselves trying to fight through the things that are consuming them. Certain words can have a profound effect on the people that they come in contact with. They will either drag one down or lift them up.

I know people who have had bad experiences with people from different cultures and because of it they say you can't trust any of them. You know, if you think about it that is why we have racism in the world today.

What I mean is someone has a problem with one from a different culture than they are, and they begin saying negative things about them and instead of allowing a person to form their own opinion, the decision has already been made for them.

We are not born with prejudice; it is something that is taught and learned. But imagine if such negative things were not taught; how much better the human race would be and how much better things would be.

Individuals used to say that others were keeping them down or from succeeding. If you really take a moment to consider what was being said, have you ever wondered why one would make unfavorable remarks about others achieving? Someone once made a comment that said the reason why they never moved forward was because all they ever seen and heard were negative.

Now, don't misunderstand me, you will always have someone who will say negative things and try to destroy your character, but the only person who controls your destiny is you. You can be your worst critic because you lack confidence in yourself.

But what if our president threw in the towel before running for office as a result of the negative remarks that many were saying concerning his race or his lack of experience? He could have allowed fear to detour him and give up, but instead he decided to face those critics and go for it.

He showed that his destiny was not in what others thought of him, but how he saw himself and he didn't allow stinking thinking to affect his decision in spite of the obstacles that he had to face and the end result of his belief is history or as someone else put it, totally priceless.

I remember hearing a judge say that her father went to law school and graduated, but he couldn't get a job because of his race. Her father could have started complaining and making excuses, but he chose not to because this man had the final say so of his destiny while setting the example to his children that all things can be achieved. So what excuses are you continuing to use for not reaching greatness in your life?

As believers, do we believe what we quote concerning the bible with words like "I can do all things through Christ who strengthen me," and "if we do, why continue to still hold on to things that we have no control of?"

So this brings me to the question concerning if we had to stand before this God, that we claim to know and love so much, what grade would he give us concerning the love we show toward our fellow man or what do you honestly think your grade would be?

Can you say that he would be pleased with the way you are at present or would you be like the rich young ruler who walked away sorrowfully? That is something to think about, huh?

We have a choice in choosing the path or directions in which we travel, but the good news is whatever choice we make, we must ask ourselves, "Am I satisfied with the path that I have traveled? Or does this describe the person that I really am? And if this is the person that I have become, what can I do to make change?"

Chapter Five

VISITING THE PERSON WITHIN

Confronting Oneself

 Moving ahead can sometimes be a difficult or challenging thing to do, especially when a person doesn't admit their wrong or take responsibility for the ugliness that they have contributed in past relationships.

 Someone once said that one of the most difficult things in life to do is admitting your own wrongness. Admitting that you are wrong is not only embarrassing, but it makes one face the reality that their behavior has affected someone in not such a good way.

 It's like that spouse who tells the family that they are going to pick up bread from the store, but at the same time know that they have no intentions of coming back. Some figure, taking the easy way out is better than dealing with the reality while failing to realize the mess that they left behind is still waiting for them. Sooner or later, we will all have to deal with our yesterday mishaps in order to fully move forward.

 It isn't always an easy task when one has to confront the disappointments that have been brought on by someone else without feeling some sort of anger as they try to figure out why this individual would betray or take advantage of them.

Visiting the Person Within

Confronting the person within without right direction can be devastating and costly when getting even is the only thing on a person's mind without understanding and neglecting the consequences that will follow.

I remember having this conversation with someone who was close to me but has now passed on. He began to express his hurts and feelings to a few of us who were very close to him one night in a meeting. I became so moved that I didn't ask him to stand up, but I took him by the hand and told this great man to get up.

I took him to the mirror and I asked this successful man what he see and he began to explain as everyone else watched in amazement, as he begin to release things that had been dormant for a long time.

He became like that bottle of soda that had been shaken up and when the lid was opened, something released from him like never before. The tears began to flow uncontrollably from many years of pain and hurt that he had encountered from his childhood throughout his adult life from those he loved and trusted the most. What an experience for everyone who was present that night because some or most of his pain everyone could relate to.

As friend, if I was able to face my giants of disappointments, surely I could help him face those negative giants that were determined to continue to show him the failures in his life instead of the successful accomplishments. This is what it is all about, when we release past hurts we can help someone else reach their full potential.

I heard a song one day on a radio station and the words really caught my attention and caused me to think. The words were, "I'm starting with the man in the mirror and I'm asking him to change his ways." It's not an everyday thing when one acknowledges their shortcomings and see the need to make some adjustments in their lives.

"In Your Journey Lies Your Awakening"

When one takes a look in the mirror, they can see their blemishes and imperfections and then become moved by what they see. As long as one can see his or her deformities, spots, and ugliness, they can try to do something about them. If one goes away from the mirror, they forget and their imperfections no longer bother them.

Or they become like the witch who deceived herself, thinking that she was the fairest of them all until she was confronted with the truth or the story of Pinocchio who couldn't see himself and the more he wasn't honest with himself, the more ridiculous he looked.

As long as one remains mindful, they can see themselves for who they really are and constantly seek to improve themselves, but if they move from seeing themselves in the mirror for what they have really become, now they become like a scripture I read that says what matter of man is this or who is this person?

Better yet, when one stops seeing themselves, they lose touch with the reality of who they are and what they have become. Sometimes trying to get people to change their behaviors or ways until they can see themselves is a losing battle.

It reminded me of the Apostle Paul when he said, "Oh, wretched man that I am, who shall deliver me?" In other words, he saw the error of his ways and realized that he needed to make a change in his life for the better or before it's too late.

I was reading how the woman who was a Canaan desired the Lord and the disciples wanted to send her away, but because she saw her need, she said even the dogs desire to eat the crumbs that fall from the master's table. You see, when one comes to grips with themselves, they don't make excuses or blame others. They just want to know how to be set free for the better.

If some of us could just stop finding excuses and come to the reality that it is me that is in need of a change or attitude adjustment, how easy out lives would be. I heard someone say excuses are useless because they don't change your tomorrow, but excuses can make your tomorrow worse than it was yesterday.

Just look at Adam when God asked him where he was. He began to play the blame game by saying the woman that he was given, gave him and he did eat. What he should have said was, "God, I disobeyed you and I'm sorry, forgive me," but instead he chose to give one excuse after another, making the matter worse than it already was.

While failing to acknowledge that the instructions concerning the tree of knowledge of good and evil were given directly to him and because he failed or neglected to see his part in the whole matter, the very thing that was given to him for safe keeping he lost.

Similar to many of us who refuse to take responsibility for our behaviors, we will find ourselves losing out on some of the most important things we have been blessed to obtain.

Bitterness

As a result of disappointment and betrayal, that thing called bitterness which is like a frozen form of latent anger. Resentment begins to grow out of refusal to let go when someone or something is taken from us which is brought on by an unpleasant memory and a constant hurt which only not grips and takes hold but it takes root.

Bitterness is the unhealthiest emotion you can have when you are offended or disappointed by others, and that individual allows the hurt to germinate in their heart as resentment takes root. Someone characterized bitterness as an unforgiving spirit, generally negative along with critical attitudes. Bitterness and resentment are both sinful and self-defeating. Perhaps it grows from the literal loss of a loved one or income or a relationship.

Sometimes it might be more subtle as it grows from the loss of a reputation or social position in a group. Whatever the cause, bitterness grows out of unreleased loss. It is a known fact that whenever we lose something or someone significant, we often feel the following thoughts and emotions over a period of time as we grieve over the loss, but bitterness pervades everything.

The question was asked, "What happens to a person if they continue to hold on to bitterness and don't let it go for years? What happens to them physically? Can they get physically sick?" Suppose it is bitterness toward some member of the family and they kept it inside nurturing it and they have not shared it. They have not confined in people—they have kept it down inside. And now after many years, something is triggered and finally the pain begins to surface.

Bitterness is one of the most destructive and dangerous of all human emotions and if one doesn't deal with it, it will destroy the person. It is the feeling of hurt, resentment, anger and even hate that can build up in our hearts when we have been hurt by another person or by life experiences and if one is not careful, their bitterness will not only be toward those that abuse them, but toward those who try to help them and toward their God as well. You see, a bitter person is his or her own worst enemy.

The concept of mental bitterness comes from the idea of something that has a sharp or unpleasant taste, especially if it brings grief.

I remember receiving a call a few years ago informing me that my oldest sister was brutally attacked and the circumstances that lead to it. My first response was I couldn't believe it and was this some sort of joke. But after arriving to the hospital and seeing the devastation on my parents faces, the reality became real.

Visiting the Person Within

The reality of losing the person who was responsible for us and was our protector when our parents went out could be leaving this world was a frightening reality.

Watching my father who always seemed to be in control no matter what, always having the last word on everything, become a man that was broken and helpless as tears rolled down his face and my mother who has always in my opinion, been the backbone of this family and could get a prayer through when no one else could was silent brought about an anger in me. I couldn't take away their pain and maybe this was because the family for some reason had this idea that I was always the calm one and that if anybody can get to the root of a thing, it would be me.

But unfortunately, I was at a loss. The more helpless I became, the more frustrated I was. My frustration went from anger to rage as bitterness began to grip me and the more I watched my sister lie helpless, the bitterer and more enraged I became.

Day in and day out watching her have to learn how to do the simple things that use to be second nature to her like bruising her teeth, dressing herself and learning how to walk all over again became more and more overwhelming as my anger and bitterness begin to get the upper hand, especially when she told me what she remembered. If my bitterness could have been on trial, I would have been found guilty in a court of law.

But the reality was that I needed to release the thing that was the culprit of my pain. Often in life, people hurt us, take advantage of us, betray us and even take the credit for what someone else has done.

Sometimes people will degrade others to elevate themselves with no regard of the other person feelings even when one hasn't done anything to deserve such treatment.

Now that seed begins to grow and many times, the person who hurts you does it unintentionally, being insensitive to what they did or said, but sometimes it is deliberate. Bitterness affects people by what is done to them, by what is said about them and from what is taken from them, and that is where the boiling point begins.

I read that the boiling point corresponds to the temperature at which the vapor pressure of the liquid equals the surrounding environment pressure and is dependent on the pressure like bitterness; when it overtakes us, there is no looking back because the pressure has become overwhelming and is at its boiling point.

I remember reading how David was bitter toward Nabal because he refused to help him and his army of men so much that he set out to kill everyone connected to Nabal, but thank God for Abigail who was the voice of reasoning. We as a people, when we are holding on to stuff that happened to us in the past, need an Abigail that will help us see the bigger picture and many innocent people wouldn't be hurt by our actions.

The Results of Bitterness

Bitterness and resentments makes one foolish, it provokes people to do and say stupid things that hurts us. Someone described bitterness as an emotional suicide and said it's like drinking poison while hoping the other person will suffer as it takes its slow time in destroying one's peace of mind by prolonging the hurt and making everyday life miserable.

Normally, bitter people have an amazing memory for the tiniest detail and they wallow in self-pity while keeping a record of every offense. It is a destructive and self-destructive power. It can be physically as well as emotionally debilitating.

Persistent bitterness and resentment makes one angry and confused. It causes fatigue, backaches, ulcers, headaches and drains our vitality. Bitterness spreads easily like a cancer that can start at stage one and escalate quickly to a stage four when not treated in time as the question of whether one will survive it or not arises.

Untreated bitterness will spread and attach itself to anyone who's in close range as it breaks down and destroy anyone that is in its path for no reason of their own.

Unfortunately, the person who is releasing such abuse will hopefully come to the conclusion that they are hurting themselves more than the other person.

Bitterness causes the person who holds it harm, it robs one's peace of mind, but most of all, it will hurt one's pride. Often, one will find themselves thinking about the person who harmed them more than they can keep count while reliving yesterday's pain and reopening old wounds that bring nothing but grief. It would seem as if one has become hooked like a drug to that person because they can't seem to shake it nor move on with their life.

Their every thought is on what the person has done to them or someone that they loved similar to the bitterness that I had toward the person who had my father in tears and my mother upset, not to mention the hell that my sisters and brothers were going through as well as her children and the rest of the family.

Bitterness will make one pessimistic and negative and if one is not careful, bitterness will and can cause stress at the same time, ruining one's health.

I read a statement that said not every sick person is bitter, but every bitter person will eventually get sick. Why? Because depression sets in and robs one of the ability to deal with day to day tasks as they find themselves slipping deeper into their own bondage, not realizing that they can be set free.

I've heard so many excuses from people who try to explain why things aren't going well for them or why they can't succeed by making statements like they are in the shape that they are in because of helping someone.

I thought to myself how ridiculous they sound, when they are the ones who choose to make the decision to help in the first place. They weren't being forced to help, but they did it out of the kindness of their heart, so they say. Now they are complaining about doing something good as a result of yesterday's blues from bitterness experienced from someone else.

We must keep in mind that when we do what is right, our time comes that someone will remember us and lend a helping hand, but most importantly, our Heavenly Father sees all and he will reward the good that we do. But if we are not careful, our bitterness will overtake us and that thing called strife will set in and drive us in a path that can destroy us.

As I continued to listen to people make statements like, "I'm not bitter, I'm over it," and yet turn around and say from the same mouth that hell will freeze over before they see or hear from them with conviction, it is mind blowing.

They have become so numb with disappointments to the point that they no longer can see themselves and have blocked out any sound of reasoning that they have become deaf because they can't even hear themselves.

One would wonder if some people become so bitter with disappointment that they can't hear their own bitterness. If we constantly rehash things from the past, such as disappointments and regrets, we will find ourselves trapped.

I heard someone make a statement one day that disturbed me because they were blaming and labeling other people like those people who hurt them. So I said to them, "How insensitive you are when these people are the ones who are helping you, and because you are having a bad day, this is how you show your appreciation." You know, bitterness, if we are not careful, can adversely affect others as well as ourselves.

Someone wrote a passage that said each individual has his or her own areas of bitterness to work on. So if we are adding our bitterness to other people who are dealing with their own issues, well, we get the point.

The good book tells us to get rid of all bitterness, rage and anger, brawling and slander, along with every form of malice. We must be kind and compassionate to one another, forgiving each other, just as Christ had forgiven us.

Many believers will quote the 12th Chapter of Hebrews, but only a few apply this to their everyday living which says, "See to it that no one misses the grace of God and that no bitter root grows up to develop trouble and defile many." Believe it or not, how we respond to situations does affect other people in our lives.

I remember having an issue with a family member because they were telling people, to my surprise, that I was not related to them. So in order to protect myself, I began to make statements that I should not have made even though I thought that I was right by protecting myself.

My statements had such a negative effect on my oldest son that when I tried to explain to him that it was my problem and not his, he wasn't hearing that.

Now the reality of my behavior was staring me right in the face and all I could do was drop my head in shame. I realized that because of my bitterness that I wasn't willing to own up to, has now affected my son.

Many times when asked about my faith, like many others, I am proud to openly confess that I am a believer of righteousness and believe that one should love their neighbor and will teach boldly on love, respect and forgiveness. But now I find myself being confronted with doing the things that I encourage others to do.

I began to think about the story of Jonah, how the passengers that were on the ship were minding their own business when Jonah brought his problem on the ship and everyone was affected and as a people, that is what we do.

Strife

Now I had to face the truth of knowing that my bitterness had stirred up strife between my son and this family member. I had to do something about it and take full responsibility because it was me who needed to get things right and not my son. The thing that my son was dealing with made me realize that I created this problem, not him.

Understanding Proverbs became clearer as I began to read how reckless words pierce like a sword, but the tongue of the wise brings healing. The Proverb also tells us to cast out the scorner and contention shall go out, yea, strife and reproach shall cease.

I began to realize that my disappointment with this family member brought about anger. My anger stirred up strife and I desire to do what is right to the best of my ability and God being my helper. I had to look within myself and not only acknowledge some truths about me, but also to make some changes in my life.

There was no need for me to try to play dumb when I knew I was the reason that my son had an issue with this family member. Unfortunately trying to make steps to do the right thing became difficult as the excuses began to follow.

I started remembering this old song that said starting all over again is going to get hard, so hard, but I'm going to make it.

That is when I started making things right by first asking my Heavenly Father to forgive me, because I believe if a person repents that they will be forgiven and I was the one who dragged my son in my mess anyway.

It doesn't matter what excuse I might have used, the truth still remains that it wasn't my son's problem but mine, and that's when the hardest part began.

What I mean is now I had to set the example with the purest of heart and call this family member up. I quickly

Visiting the Person Within

learned that holding on to bitterness and strife is not so easy to get rid of, especially when you feel that you are innocent and hadn't wronged anyone and for me it was the truth as well as difficult.

I felt like Paul when he said, "The thing that I should do is the thing that I don't do and the thing that I shouldn't do is the thing that I do."

The thing that I was doing was speaking very negative about it instead of confronting the issue as one thing led to another. But when he said that the reason he couldn't do the thing that he should do was because of the law of sin dwelling with him, I knew I had to get it right.

So I called this family member up and I asked them to forgive me. I explained that I was wrong for the statements that I made concerning them.

And to my surprise, it was as if they wanted me to get out of character and a part of me wanted to get out of character because, in my opinion, they were just being as difficult and bull headed as one can get and to add insult to injury, they began making statements like, "Are you sick and dying," or, "Are you trying to make peace with your God," as they begin to laugh like this was some sort of joke as they continued to enquire if I was dying and needed to get things right.

I had to keep Proverbs 15:1 before me that says that a gentle answer turns away wrath, but a harsh word stirs up anger.

You talk about eating humble pie. I kept my cool, but it wasn't as easy as I thought, and before I hung my phone up, I told them that I loved them and that I was very sorry. I must say it was a challenge, but I was so glad that I took that stand because, for whatever reason I had or didn't have, I was responsible for the way my son was feeling.

Many of us are guilty for how our loved ones or friends feel toward people that we have made unfavorable remarks about in their presence.

Just like Jonah, because he did not do that which was right, everyone around him was affected when they had nothing to do with it. And that is what we do, get other people involved in our issues of negativity, giving them room to react on a matter that is pure gossip that has nothing to do with them.

Maybe we as a people should try to keep Proverbs 13:3 in mind that says, "He that keepeth his mouth keepeth his life: but he that openeth wide his lips shall have destruction." This is similar to many of us who have allowed our disappointments to have such a negative effect in our lives that we say things that we shouldn't.

We have people involved in our issues that need to be minding their own business, but instead, we have planted a seed that is unfavorable toward someone which has opened a door for others to have an opinion about something they really know nothing about.

We continuing to justify ourselves by making statements like, "I tried to get things right, but the individuals made it so difficult for me, so I left it alone."

With all honesty, we left it alone, but we sort of had a bump it type of attitude, but I say take it a step further and ask our Heavenly Father to forgive us because we did get a little upset when the person wouldn't hear us. I say let's get rid of bitterness and strife so that all of us can grow and become the persons we are destined to be.

If you or someone that you know is really trying to be set free from this bondage of bitterness, I'd like to recommend this prayer that I read. The writer of this prayer is unknown, but I added some things and made it my own because it was a blessing as well as a help to me and I know it will be a blessing to all that is ready to close the door on yesterday's unpleasantness and open the door of today's possibilities.

Father, life seems so unjust and so unfair. The pain of rejection is almost more than I can bear. My past relationships ended in strife, anger, rejection, and separation. Lord, I know that you can provide me with instructions on how to let go of all bitterness and indignation, wrath and resentment. You are the one who binds up and heals the broken-hearted. I receive your anointing that destroys every yoke of bondage.

I receive emotional healing by faith and I thank you for giving me the grace to stand firm until the process is complete. I choose, as an act of my will, to forgive and I ask that you forgive them as well and not hold these charges against him or her on my account and if there be any more stored up negative feelings in me toward anyone, I asked that you cleanse me and help me regain the ground that I gave up when I held onto these offenses. I ask that you heal now the wounded places in my soul. Please heal my memory of those offenses so that I can look back on them realistically knowing that you have healed me. I ask that you may bless them with your abundant mercy.

Thank you for wise counselors. I acknowledge the Holy Spirit as my wonderful counselor. Thank you for helping me work out my salvation with fear and trembling for it is you, Father, who works in me to will and to act according to your good purpose.

In the name of my Heavenly Father, I choose to forgive those who have wronged me. I purpose to live a life of forgiveness because you have forgiven me.

With the help of the Holy Spirit, I get rid of all bitterness, rage, anger, brawling and slander along with every form of malice. I desire to be kind and compassionate to others, forgiving them just as, Christ, you forgave me.

With the help of the Holy Spirit, I make every effort to live in peace with all men and to be holy for I know that without holiness no one will see you, Lord. I purpose to see to it I do not miss your grace and that no bitter root rise up within me to cause trouble.

I will watch and pray that I enter not into temptation or cause others to stumble. Thank you, Father that you watch over your word to perform it and that the son that you have set free is free indeed. I declare that I have overcome resentment and bitterness by the blood of the Lamb and by the word of my testimony. Amen.

My desire and hope for whoever reads this prayer is that each day or every other day you allow yourself to be released from bitterness, hatred and strife because you are better than that.

Each pound of this negative weight that you release will allow you to come closer to redemption sooner than you think.

Chapter Six

HOW татоP THE HURTING

*P*eople often say they want to be able to let go and move on but they just don't know how. They say that they have invested so much in the relationship. It is just so hard to walk away. Many would say that it is just too hard to let go and release all the pain and disappointments that they have encountered from past relationships.

The question was asked concerning how one heals or what it means to be healed. Is it possible to start over again? According to Webster, to heal means to make sound or whole, to cause to be overcome, to patch up, to restore to original purity or integrity.

I was talking to someone not long ago and they were explaining to me that they know they needed to forgive, but they don't know how. They begin to tell me that the deception was just too painful to bear. They tied to understand how someone can say that they love you, However at the same time betray you and put all the blame on an individual without taking any responsibility, it is just a bit too much.

They wanted to know how to forgive a spouse who had an affair and a child is the result of it. Or what about a husband or wife who gets you hooked on drugs and turns your family against you? They began to say that the pain is just too hard to deal with. How is it possible that they can move on with their lives like they did nothing wrong?

There are so many that have this report or something similar concerning hurt and disappointments. Needless to say many have been wounded in one way or another by people they have loved and trusted.

While listening to what was being said, I began to wonder within my thoughts that maybe we sometimes put our all in to someone so quickly. We neglect to take it slow by surrendering totally, and when we fall, there is no cushion waiting to catch us as the hurt from the drop can be excruciating.

This is not a bad thing because as human beings we desire or like to believe that there is no reason why we can't trust those that we love. We become so caught up with our beliefs that sometimes we forget that people have short comings and imperfections. Several warning signs can be staring us right in the face, but we still neglect or refuse to pay attention to the warning signs because we don't want to proceed with caution.

We want what we want and if family and best friends try to warn us with their interventions, all drama as one would say will break loose because our minds are set. We don't want to believe and will not believe someone we love could ever do anything to hurt us until it's too late.

I know people who refuse to deal with their moms and dads because their parents were right about something that they did not want to hear.

Best friends for many years fall out with one another over relationships they disapprove of, but this doesn't change the fact that their pain is real.

But the question still remains on the table: how does the healing process begin when there is so much anger and hurt?

It reminds me of the person that I was talking to. They said that the person who hurt them publically asked them to please forgive them. But they couldn't let it go, yet they knew within themselves that they wanted to be free of the hurt and disappointment.

It has been said that we as a people sometimes have a need to want to hold on to something that is not there because of the reality that we have created within. Now realizing that the truth has surfaced and having to deal with the shame becomes unbearable as our lives are turned upside down, while a part of us is hoping that the person is just going through something and that they will come to their senses.

Some believe that if they make changes within themselves or lose some weight that things would get better. We sometimes develop false expectations concerning people that we are in relationship with. Letting go is the hardest thing for many people to do. But, it is the best thing if we are serious about healing.

The key to healing begins within oneself. What I mean is we must first look at the affect that it has on our lives. This is sometimes the hardest thing to do, but it must be done. Why? If we don't become honest with ourselves, devastation will set in and one will begin acting in ways that are totally out of their character.

Some scream and yell for no apparent reason while neglecting themselves as they continue to find reasons to justify excessive drinking, not remembering where it began or how it will end as depression sets in and take over.

I have heard of women who check all their husbands and boyfriends messages because of their insecurities in the relationship. They will take it upon themselves to call every unfamiliar number. Many will go on a hunt and as soon as they spot that man, you'll think a riot was breaking out from all the loud cussing and swearing that was going on, totally out of control and not caring who sees them or knows about what they are going through because to them this is acceptable behavior.

There are men who rent cars, acting like they are private investigators disguising themselves in order to see who their wives or girlfriends are hanging around with because of their jealousy. They demonstrate uncontrollable behaviors, believing that embarrassing her makes him look good but the truth is, it doesn't matter who is at fault because when such behavior is displayed; people develop their own opinion and will make statements like, "With that behavior, I would leave them, too."

I was reading in the book of Proverbs, and it said that for as churning the milk produces butter and as twisting the nose produces blood, so stirring up anger produces strife. Hot words stir up strife, so one must try to control themselves because if one continues on biting and devouring each other, eventually they will be destroyed by one another.

Cain's jealousy towards his brother turned into bitterness, hatred and murder. It's important to have control over the words that come out of our mouths because they can be very destructive and cause a lot of damage too many people, especially the innocent.

You might ask what does this have to do with your healing. The response to that question would be that if one doesn't confront the anger and rage that lies within them, there will be no healing because every time that individual's name is mentioned, bitterness will surface and become like a termite just eating away at them until it tears one down.

If one hasn't reached a state of forgiveness, being near to the person who hurt them may be tense and stressful as well as unhealthy.

Unfortunately, there are so many stories concerning husbands, wives, boyfriends, and girlfriends who have separated. Because the children look like the father or mother, those children were physically, mentally and even verbally abused.

Some parents go to the point of even kidnapping their own children just to get back at their spouses because the one or the other never came to grips with their pain and hurt. They will do whatever it takes to get back at the individual by whatever means are necessary, even if it means turning their children against their parents.

There have been devastating reports of people who refuse to receive counseling, and as a result of not getting the necessary help that they sincerely need. They take that same pain in new relationships only to keep ending up in the same situation and never coming to grips that they are the problem.

It has been said that the reason why some second and third marriages don't work is because the parties never recovered from their past hurts from their first marriage.

It's like a person who has a serious drinking problem and is in denial until reality kicks in. They come to grips with the fact that they have a problem and acknowledge that they are an alcoholic. Now the recovery process can begin.

Similar to one who is hurting and trying not to be so tough, or in denial, but acknowledges that the hurt and pain is too much to handle and asks for help then the healing process can begin.

Let the healing began

Healing begins with releasing the thing that is causing the most pain in one's life, such as resentment, regret and stress. Since there is no magic stick that we can pull out of a hat and the problem disappears, one must come face to face with the reality of what caused the breakdown then accept the fact that the problems didn't happen overnight and realize that neither will the healing process happen overnight.

It's like having an illness or sickness and not knowing what is really causing the problem until many exams are taken and only then can the right treatment for the illness begin along with the right prescription.

Even with the right prescription, it still takes time for the medication to start working. Often with the right medication, it might take a second or third visit back to their physician to get a stronger dosage. This is similar to being hurt; when one comes to the reality of why the breakup was so devastating then the right remedy can begin.

There are good remedies that can be done in order to have a fresh start or have a new beginning, but only the right remedy will work.

Step 1

Starting With One Self

When one is internally angry and bitter, it doesn't take much for the fuse to be lit. It's the little things that make no sense that can really set things off. Being disappointed and let down can create emotions and behaviors that the average person would never imagine experiencing.

Just like the alcoholic who says, "I'm not addicted! I'm in full control," until they are confronted with a crisis. They are being faced with all sorts of emotions while temptation is facing them hard and if they can't get in touch with someone quickly, they will slip back into some old behaviors that can become very costly to them.

Because the reality is as long as one doesn't have to face people that have hurt them or disappointed them, they feel that they don't have a problem and will make comments that the other person has a problem and not them until they come face to face with those they thought they have forgiven and those old feelings surface and all one can say is, "uh oh."

Now the reality is this: who is going to be the bigger person? Having a mind setting of revenge and not thinking clearly can result in many regrets and wrong decisions and now here comes the statement of if I could do it over again, or if I had another chance or opportunity, I would do things differently.

A person addicted to anger will have judgment issues to the point that any excuse for their actions is acceptable to them. They believe that they have a right to go the heck off on any given Sunday because of what was done to them. They make statements like, "You don't know what they did to me" and "How they wronged me."

Or their famous line about how their parents disowned them and for God sake let's not forget about those so called church people who deceived them. Or better yet, it was the hot chocolate that I drank that just set everything off. Just one more excuse to justify uncontrollable behavior.

It's amazing how some people have faced devastating heart breaks in their lives and finds the willpower and strength within them self to pick up the pieces and turn their tragedy into something great, while others are determined to make other people's lives a living hell with revenge.

I believe I either saw a movie or it's possible I read this in a book about a young man who killed the son of a Christian family. As I recall, somehow this young man was being mentored by the dead son's parents to the point that they had this young man over to their home for dinner and entreated him as their very own.

It was stated that this young man's conscience bothered him so bad that he decided to tell them and face the consequence. To the young man's surprise, the family was hurt and angry, but they chose to forgive him and allow him to have a fresh start in life.

Some would say these people had a right to be unforgiving as well as angry, but they took lemons and made lemonade. There are so many examples that we all can learn from like the young man who went on a shooting spree, hurting and taking the lives of innocent people, but their families were able to forgive him.

Every day, some parent somewhere is put in a situation with their children that causes them so much pain and disappointments, but something within them gives them the strength to support them and be there for them when others would say those kids need to be responsible for their actions.

That is a true saying, but because some parents remembered their past mistakes and have been forgiven from maybe their parents or others when they didn't deserve it, they haven't forgotten that they were forgiven while others continued to act like they never did anything wrong.

Some women who have been violated must deal with the reality that as a result of such abuse, a child has been conceived, but something within them or an inner strength allows them to have a child that was not conceived by love, but love that child unconditionally and will refuse to allow anyone to say anything to that child that would bring about hurt and shame.

After teaching and letting that child know that they are a blessing and that none of this was their fault, they are in amazement.

Husbands and wives can find love again with one another after much hurt. But most importantly, how about our Lord and Savior that was crucified for crimes he didn't commit but yet ask his Heavenly Father to forgive them for they know not what they do.

We can also learn from people such as family and friends that are close to us who have had bad experiences, gone through more drama than one can imagine and find it within themselves to move forward, while many that are close to them do nothing but fault find and make comments concerning what they would or would not do. But because they made the decision to turn negativity into a positive, they have a peace of mind and are showing others that all things are possible if they want it.

But the question is this: Are you ready to come face to face with yourself and begin a new chapter? In other words, are you ready to enter into your full potential of destiny?

Step 2

Getting Started

Coming face to face with oneself is the beginning of a fresh start. Becoming sick and tired of being fed up and eager to do something about it? When one comes to the conclusion that they are overweight and it is affecting their health, they just don't talk about it, but they do something about it.

A person who knows that they need to stop smoking don't continue making excuses on how hard it is to quit; they will start wearing a nicotine patch or chew gum to carve the cravings. I heard that some just go cold turkey because their health is more important to them than lying on a sick bed with breathing tubes.

Take a person for instance who always gets in trouble for hanging out with the wrong crowd even though they are not doing anything, but the company that they associate themselves with is bad news.

They come to the conclusion that even though they have been friends with these individual since they were children and they don't have a problem with them, but if they don't stop hanging with them, they will be in jail or dead.

So they tell their friends, "I don't have issues with you all at all, but I can't afford to keep getting in trouble and missing out on opportunities because of who they're connected to" and they leave not allowing the negative words to affect their decision.

Getting started starts with accepting the fact that a change needs to take place in order to move from one point to a greater point. Just like a person who is afraid of height, they know in order to overcome it they must confront it.

But the question is: what is keeping us from taking that first step? Is it possible that the reality of fear has set in because of not knowing what to expect. But what is fear? Fear is being afraid or apprehensive, viewing the future with anxiety or alarm. There is nothing wrong with being a little apprehensive or cautious, but I heard someone use the illustration of a person being in a car accident.

They said that the more a person procrastinates as a result of an accident and allows fear to grip them, the longer it will take for them to face the reality that they can win back their lives and gain control. But if a person gets back behind the wheel quickly, it will help them overcome the fear quicker and gain control back over their lives.

It's like coming to a cross road and trying to figure out which path to take, wanting to get started but just not knowing how because of the fear of the unknown.

There was a story about two farmers and it was said that both of them needed it to rain, but only one of them went out and prepared the ground for the rain. The other one, due to the fear of failure, wouldn't prepare the ground for the rain. When the rain came, the one who didn't prepare remained where he was while the other reaped the benefits. There comes a time in all of our lives that, in spite of past experience, we must develop blind-like faith in order to have a fresh start and just go for it.

Step 3

Facing the Unknown

In order to become free from the thought of failure, one must begin to become mobile or active again by facing their fear, feeling that unpleasant, often strong emotion caused by anticipation or loss of courage. That thing called fear will bring about dread which usually adds the idea of intense reluctance to face or meet a person, or situation and suggests aversion as well as anxiety.

Fear is like imprisonment; it has you confined to a place where hope seems impossible, bound and chained behind bars that you can see out of but can't get out of while having a firm grip when one gives into it. We know that people say fear is false evidence appearing real because ninety percent of the things we fear never happen, but if we become overwhelmed with fear, that thing called failure will kick in.

Failure is one of the dirtiest words in our society— including all the four letter words. Most people would rather be odd, hostile, overworked, or many other "terrible" things than be seen as a failure.

To come to grips with the reasons why we feel pressure or anxiety about failure, we have to understand that it is the fear of failure that hurts far more than the failure itself. Truthfully, it is the fear of not being sure what will happen. Most of us can learn to accept and deal with the worst if we really know what's coming. We may not like it, but we can handle it. Each of us is different in the things we fear and to analyze the reasons we are pressured by the fear of failure, we have to find out what kinds of failure bother us.

To overcome fear, it is important to be completely aware of the thoughts and feelings driving it. Only then will freedom be realized. Someone once said that you know what you got, but you don't know what you are going to get.

But I say if we stop being a slave to fear that the possibility on the other side can be joy unspeakable. We must break down that wall of fear because it is blocking us from reaching our full potential.

When fear becomes our roommate, we see no hope or exit out because we have made walls with no windows or doors.

It reminds me about a story I heard concerning this Indian boy who the doctor said would never walk and in order for his mother to keep him close to her, she made a box and put him in it with a rope tied around her waist so that he wouldn't be far from her. She dragged him in this box everywhere she went, but like most children, this young boy had a lot of energy. He would be rocking that box from side to side and his mother would panic with fear and yell at him to stop.

She was so fearful of him hurting himself that she couldn't see any possibility of him walking, or even visualizing the idea that there might be a possibility that he could walk. But as for her son, he wasn't thinking about what she was thinking. To allow that thing called fear to be his stumbling block was not in his radar because all he could see was the window of opportunity.

So one day while his mother was in the kitchen preparing dinner, he decided enough already of being in this box and he knocked the box completely over by rocking back and forth with conviction; he controlled his fear, and the fear of the unknown had no rule over him.

He was able to rock that box over and crawl out of it. He didn't allow fear to grip him but he gripped it, and I guess one would say he saw the glass half full instead of half empty.

No one knows, what will happen when they venture out from the box. Knocking the box over will open up avenues that seem impossible. Kicking the box over doesn't show you your potential for today, but it show's you your possibilities for tomorrow. I believe that if we do the best we can do, God will do the rest.

Freedom

Someone said that freedom is the quality or state of being free, as the absence of necessity, coercion, or constraint in choice or action. To be liberated from restraint or from the power of another, or to be released from something, but many people will let the fear of failure hinder them and it does. It stops them from reaching their full potential as well as reaching for new goals. It also keeps them from taking advantage of new opportunities and living life to its fullness.

To overcome fear, it is important to be completely aware of the thoughts and feelings driving it. Only then will freedom be realized. A good illustration of this is a salesman who knows that for every sale he makes, he will get ten rejections. He can take the easy way out and say, "I'll try maybe again tomorrow because it looks like I'm probably not going to be able to do anything today, so I might as well knock off" or he can say," One down, only nine to go until I make my sale." The latter will keep him on the job longer with a much more satisfying feeling and better sales.

There are many people who have dreams and hopes of becoming successful, but the follow through becomes difficult for them. When asked why one wouldn't pursue their dreams or take the necessary steps toward their success, believe it or not, it all balls down to fear of not being able to accomplish what they have started.

Some believe that their past would interfere with their future. But I say if that be the case, the majority of people would never reach their full potential because most didn't have or come from humble beginnings. Their parents weren't billionaires who left huge inheritance to just ordinary people who worked hard and hoped for the best. Some have had one parent or no parents but had a desire to do better for themselves and took a leap of faith.

Can you just image a woman like Rosa Parks who one day became fed up? There were probably many that might have thought about it, but she was the only one who stood up and didn't allow fear to overpower her.

I can only imagine the challenges that she had to face not only with the opposition, but with her peers and her own race. Many tried to discourage her by telling her to leave it alone because she was not only going to get herself killed, but she was making matters uncomfortable for everyone else. But what they failed to realize was that when the why is big enough, the facts don't count.

Being free or having freedom applies not only to material things, but it also in my opinion, applies to having an inner confidence in one's self. Just like in the Special Olympics, in spite of the challenge that many encounter as a result of their disabilities, they have courage and confidence in themselves and they make it happen by not using their handicaps to interfere in their accomplishments and to me that is truly freedom.

Being able to love and respect yourself regardless of whether you live on Main Street or Wall Street with one loaf of bread or one slice of bread because you know it won't be like this always is freedom.

Freedom is not measured upon what one has, but it is what one believes. It is the state of being at liberty rather than being in confinement and having the ability to make choices.

An individual can have everything but at the same time live in an invisible prison that they have built in their own mind by having a fear of not being able to maintain it and the results can be devastating.

This same scenario can apply to another person who can barely make the ends to meet, just having enough to make it from one week to the next but finds strength to have an inner peace. The difference between the two is one has a fear of maintaining while the other chose not to dwell on things that they can't control.

Someone said dreams, aspiration, as well as ideas, mean nothing if one does not have the freedom and courage to pursue them. I have watched movies where a person was stranded and had nothing, but they took their mind to a place and the next thing you saw was them being under fresh running water. What an inner peace for someone to have because if one won't believe in something better than what they have, things will remain the same.

It reminds me of what I learned concerning the house slave and the field slave. It was stated that the house slave way of thinking was that they had all the freedom that they needed because master, in their mind, was good to them, so they became comfortable and forgot that they were not free but were brought for a price and owned by master.

As a result of this, they became comfortable and stopped believing in freedom and yielded to their circumstances. But on the other hand, the field slave never forgot where they were and why they were there. They could taste freedom so bad that they didn't allow anything or anyone to get in the way. In order to reach destiny, one must free themselves from their own bondage of imprisonment.

I'm reminded of the children of Israel who finally were freed from Egypt but still in chains in their minds. When things didn't go their way, they began to reflect back to when they were in Egypt while neglecting the reason why they wanted to leave Egypt. They left Egypt, but that Egypt mentality was still very much a part of them.

One would ask the question concerning what you do when you come to a crossroad in your life and there is a fork in the road and it's now decision making time, but you find yourself in a paralyzed state. You know what is on the right, but there is a block in the road, and you don't know what's on the left.

You begin to wonder within yourself what your next move should be, but caution sits in and now you begin reflecting on what were familiar verses, what the possibilities can be, like the children of Israel. When they came out of Egypt, they came to a crossroad and began to talk about what they had instead of seeing what they were about to get.

They forgot about how difficult it was for them and how they prayed for freedom, but because the road ahead appeared to be troublesome, it didn't take much for them to quickly reflect back and develop amnesia.

They reminded me of that old saying that states you can take the boy out of the country but not the country out of the boy. You can remove one from their environment, but if they keep the same mind setting, that old environment is still living inside of them and it doesn't matter where they go.

One must never forget when there is a fork in the road, it only means that the choice you make will determine if you remain a prisoner in your mind or are you one of many that have been released from that bondage of blockage in one's own mind while visualizing new found freedom?

Having a fresh start in life depends on how bad one wants to stop the bleeding in their lives that causes them so much pain and discomfort. We are responsible for what we do, say, think and feel as we must come to the conclusion and accept the fact that we have no control over another's negative behavior.

Then and only then will freedom begin and healing wins because the stains of the past will start washing away as signs of hope surface as one adopts the attitude that all things are possible if they would only believe by putting one foot in front of the other without looking back.

Chapter Seven

REMOVE THE TOXINS

We know that a toxin is a poison made by living cells or organisms that can cause health problems as it attacks the body with a chain reaction of unfamiliar aches and pains that can become crippling as the body breaks down.

You see, the average person usually won't associate their body's lack of health to its sources because, like toxins, holding on to grudges usually builds up within us over long periods of time.

I was reading an article that was dealing with the invisible risks of welding and it was said that the world is full of sixty year olds who regret not protecting their health when they were younger.

It is well documented that many long term health problems associated with the profession are preventable. But because the causes and incremental effects can be invisible, literally, they tend to be ignored until welders grow older and the impact of that disregard can be ignored no longer.

It is similar to many mishaps in relationships that have not been handled properly and the roots from it has grown and those branches of hurt, bitterness and disappointments have grown like wildflowers as many begin finding themselves in a dilemma.

"In Your Journey Lies Your Awakening"

Coming to the reality that after all those years and now trying to process the results can have a devastating impact because what used to be no longer exists and right when one feel they have gotten over the pain, those hidden things in us begin to surface and we wonder within ourselves where this came from.

It reminds me of a medical program one morning that I was watching concerning the seriousness of anorexia. As I continued to watch, the doctor began to talk about a man who had anorexia for more than twenty years. This was very surprising to me because you only hear talk concerning women with this problem instead of men.

This doctor began to explain how this man became so obsessed with his health that in my opinion this man lost touch with reality and it showed, even though everyone was telling him how good he looked.

There was some sort of mental blockage as he went from one extreme to another. His determination of being in the best of health for whatever reason, whether he had been picked on as a child or lacked confidence in his self, blindsided him to the point that he couldn't see that he was in serious trouble and at death's door.

This is exactly what happens when one chooses not to let go of their anger and rage; they can't see how close they are to the edge, and at any moment they can stumble and the impact from the fall can bring such devastation that only a higher power can restore.

I read a passage in the bible that said to be angry but sin not. I believe the writer was trying to warn us that if we are not careful; our anger will turn into rage along with uncontrollable behaviors that will lead to much hurt and regret as our disappointments will lead us to either becoming bitter or better and nine out of ten, it makes us bitter.

Cain's wroth with Abel caused him to murder his brother and when the Lord asked him concerning the whereabouts of his brother, he had the same attitude like most of us who have bitterness in our hearts—we really don't care and will dismiss it as if the problem doesn't exist.

But if Cain could have turned back the hands of time, he would have handled things differently. You hear many people say that they didn't mean to do what they did and if they had to do it all over again, the outcome would be different.

It's like coming to grips with the reality of knowing that unhealthy eating can cause obesity as well as hypertension and yet as a people, we continue to eat unhealthy in order to hide behind what's causing the behavior until we are faced with the dilemma of all types of life threatening health issues.

Similar too not releasing the mistreatment from someone else, one will continue to hold on to not being able to forgive as bitterness sets in.

Holding on to bitterness, strife and anger without trying to remove it in order to feel relief and have a peace of mind is like putting the wrong foods in your body. Not realizing the harm that one is doing to their health until it's too late can result too many health issues as toxins begin to build and the only way to rid those toxins is through purifying the body just to feel relief.

One must become mindful that in order to flush those toxins of resentment, bitterness and anger out of their system, they must develop a different mind setting. If not, that toxin known as depression will move in and set up residence without provision and the only way to move it out is by an eviction notice.

Truthfully, no one wakes up in the morning and says, "Today I will be depressed and mean it." But because of unresolved hurts and not being able to cope with the pain, it can bring about a rage that one would never believe that they had. Now, that thing called depression takes a hold of them and out of the blue, here comes that uninvited guest named dejection and now the party begins as sadness creeps in and takes over.

Having that feeling of closing the world out while hiding under the covers to escape creates more melancholy as family and friends struggle to find words to encourage them to no avail as hopelessness begins to take root and grow.

Now, when the question is asked, why did you or how did you? Allow the situation to get to this point? All one would hear is, "I don't know why I went back to visit or to make peace because nothing has changed and those people are the same selfish, ungrateful individuals that they have always been."

You can hear how upset and frustrated they are and when the question is asked of them, why, when you know how they are, do you stoop to their level and put yourself in that type of environment? All one would hear are statements like, "I thought after all these years that the situation would be different."

There is an old saying that states to change one of their will they are of the same opinion still. We can't change yesterday, but we can sure make a difference today because that is not this and this is not that.

It reminds me of when my father died. I kept visiting his gravesite as if I was expecting him to tell me something. At the same time, knowing that all that I didn't know, I will never know, I kept going back anyway. I guess, I was reacting like many people who, instead of leaving well enough along, continue allowing themselves to get deeper and deeper into something that really brings about no good.

I recall being in my hotel room about to leave when the phone began to ring and when I answered it, there was a pastor on the other end looking for my husband, but he had left to attend one of the seminars. As God would have it or as some would say, as fate would have it, this great woman of God began to minister unto me about things that only God and myself knew about.

Remove the Toxins

To my surprise, she began to ask me what, if anything was I expecting to hear from my deceased father from the grave. I began to ponder what she was saying because I knew looking back wasn't going to change anything. She proceeded to tell me that I needed to release it and let it go because the effect it had on me was hindering me from some great potentials.

She reminded me that looking back in my case would bring no good and that I have no control of what other people do.

It reminded me of a story that I heard concerning a scorpion and a toad. It was said that the scorpion needed to get across to the other side but needed the assistance of the toad. But the strange thing about the story is that the toad knew the nature of the scorpion and still allowed himself to be stung again as if he didn't get it the first time around.

Just like people who have insight of their past, for some usual reason they will retreat back to a situation that was unhealthy for them. It appears as if they are a glutton for a punishment, but the truth of the matter is that they have become blindsided to the reality of what it is.

Just like the toad, he knew that the scorpion could not be trusted. He even said to the scorpion, "Why take you across the river when I know that you are going to sting me?" That is the same question that we as a people need to ask ourselves. Or better yet, why do we as a people constantly do the same things, especially when the results are the same?

Similar to one that is in an abusive relationship and an inner voice is crying out warning, please don't go back. But something begins to tug at them, making them believe a lie instead of seeing the reality of what is standing in front of them until it's too late.

Now, one will find themselves spiraling out of control while trying to accept those nagging questions of why do I keep going back? I know once the thrill is gone, they are gone too, but even when one knows the facts, they will continue

"In Your Journey Lies Your Awakening"

to try to rationalize what just happened instead of listening to the part that is telling them don't do it.

Those famous words of, "I'm so sorry" blindsides one from the reality of what the truth is. But I heard someone once say that the same way we justify to remain in harm's way is more of a reason to leave, especially when one begins to question, "What does this person do for me in this relationship?"

When one has been rescued from a burning building and the firemen makes it clear that it is not safe to enter back into the building, but for some strange reason, one feels the need to ignore the advice that was given and there are devastating results because someone thought they had a better plan.

Because one might believe that they are in control of the situation and know what they are doing doesn't make it right. If that was the case, Lot's wife in the bible would not have been destroyed. But because she thought she knew what she was doing when she was advised not to look back, she became deceived and the end result was not good.

It is important to keep in mind that once the egg is cracked, we cannot say, "I changed my mind, so I am going to put the egg back together." The harder you try, the bigger the mess becomes because the pain of your past can be the blueprint of your future if one is not careful. That one look back is what causes the most pain in people lives because most would rather remain with what is familiar verses what is logical.

I'm reminded of some literature that was given to me about this man who was having a seminar. As I began to read the history of this gentleman, I learned that he had a lot of mishaps in his life. Being taken away from his mother as a child, a pass cocaine user and dealer, a failed marriage that he took responsibility for and last but not least, he had served some serious prison time.

This man could have thrown in the towel and said to himself that because he messed up so bad, what made him feel that he deserve a second chance or who in their right mind would want to give him another chance?

He made the decision that those toxins from his past would not dictate his future. As a result of not being influenced by all the negative insults concerning him, he lectures all over the world teaching others that their past is not what determines their future because whatever toxins they carried today can be cleansed tomorrow.

There was a statement made that said it's not who you are or where you came from or what you been through and it has nothing to do with how you start, but it has everything to do with how you finish. You see, the race is not given to the swift nor the strong, but to those who endure until the end. It is not in the negative words that people say concerning you, it is about the things that you do concerning you.

Someone was telling me that as a child they had been in several foster homes and that the conditions were so bad that they had to steal food in order for them and their sibling to eat. They talked about how they got involved with the wrong crowd of people, and how, according to statistics, they should have been dead or in jail. By their choice, they decided not to allow those toxins from their past to clog their future. By not allowing those toxins to infiltrate, they are very successful and well respected.

There are many toxins that have been deposited by parents to their children because one parent or both parents felt like one child wasn't as smart or as intelligent as the other. Those toxins known as abuse and shame encountered from one or both parents who constantly made statements to them like, "Why can't you be like your brother and sister" or, "Like the neighbors kid's across the street who never get in trouble and embarrass there family?"

From one extreme to next, while failing to see that the road map that they are preparing for that son or daughter—as a result of neglect and negative comments— has not only been inflicted on them, but planted. This leaves one to wonder whether or not the parents are aware that they have a responsibility of bringing up a child in the way or direction in which they should go.

Unfortunately, there are many people who continue to carry those stains of what happened years ago, continuing to function while hiding behind that veil as if everything is okay, but deep within them, they are still not releasing those memories of disappointments from toxins of hurt, anger and bitterness. They have negative thoughts and plans concerning anyone who they feel have done them wrong. Their thoughts consist of nothing less than getting even with revenge. But the question is, will getting revenge make things better or worse?

Some believe strongly that they will be feeling a whole lot better because you don't know the hell that they had to encounter from those who had confidence and faith in everyone else except for them. As far as reaping what one has sown, that will be coming directly from them because they're determined to make them pay.

This is similar to one who made sacrifices for the family, who had the belief and confidence that the struggles would soon be over and conditions would be better than they have ever been, only to come face to face with the reality that their partner has been planning not only to leave them, but to divorce them and marry someone else.

There are so many reasons why people continue to hold on to toxins from their past, not realizing that they are becoming like a system that is backing up and out of order from all the stuff that's packed in it.

I was reading a health article and it said that the solution to the pollution is dilution. It gave a clear understanding of why the body holds on to excess weight. It talked about how the body will hold on to weight to store pesticides if there is not a mechanism for safely removing them.

It's the same scenario concerning many people who have allowed many mishaps from their past to weigh them down, leaving their system backed up with unnecessary junk that they develop toxins.

Experiences that have left them in a paralyzed state, like venom from a snake when not treated in an ample time, can lead to serious consequences, as many will wake up in a place of no return, being stunned with the outcome.

Many would say, "If I could just turn the hands of time back for twenty four hours and think things through, those toxins of bitterness, rage and not letting go would not have taken such a grip on their life."

Because the reality is it wasn't that deep in the first place. But that thing called pride begins to grip one like a choke hold that they can't break free from, leaving them with many regrets as a result of so much wasted time and the reality of what it was all about makes no sense.

Now the question is: is it possible after all those years to flush all those toxins that have been inflamed and find wholeness again? And if so, what must one do to start the process?

In order for the process to begin, one must expose the toxins from the place of concealment because wholeness is the concept that we contain all potentials for our actions and thoughts.

In order to remove those toxins that have had one in a place of confinement, one must face that giant that started the process of bitterness and uneasiness in the first place. Unfortunately, this can be the most difficult thing for one to do, especially if their uneasiness is due to betrayal by one that they trusted. Because now they are faced with the question of, "How could I have been so wrong about this person?" But the truth of the matter is we all have made bad choices, but bad choices don't have to be fatal.

Being willing to accept and face the consequences while taking responsibility is a challenge for most people because accepting the consequences of our choices is not a surefire test of whether the choices we made were right or wrong.

We can and will make mistakes, but the most important part of the decisions we make is acknowledging whether one is right or wrong that we can be forgiven.

I once read that forgiveness is the freedom to make wrong choices because with forgiveness you discover that being wrong is not all that bad. And besides, if we never made mistakes in our lives, what would be our blueprint of learning and what advice could we offer to someone if we never experienced some mistakes?

One thing that I have come to believe in my own life is that no wrong choice that I have made is going to persuade God to love me any less and no wrong choice you make can persuade God to love you less than he did when you did things right.

Forgiving someone for what they have done is a gracious way to cope with personal pain. It allows one to face the facts and get a clearer understanding of the situation. We can understand the facts not by looking at an individual's behavior but by learning what the intentions were from the behavior.

It has been said that we feel facts as we interpret them and we interpret them as we feel them. We as a people interpret facts from a moral viewpoint and no one can really convince us that a person doesn't know the difference between right and wrong and the problems that they cause.

A Danish philosopher from the eighteen hundreds wrote a prayer similar to this that said: Lord, I have to make a choice and I am afraid that I may make the wrong one. But I have to make it any way and I can't put it off. So I will make it and trust you to forgive me if I do wrong. And Lord, I will trust you, too, to help me make things right afterward.

This is how we should be when we are trying to understand the facts of what caused a person to do what they did. Just maybe their decision was based upon a situation that was going to bring about devastation or worse to all parties involved. Many might say, "I know, but I just want things back the way they were. But I just don't know how to get there. Or how to feel whole after being deceived so much."

Someone once stated that it begins with forgiving oneself because the thoughts we create and whatever we believe in ourselves, is what we experience. Because in order for the process of wholeness to begin, we must be honest with whatever role we might have had by asking God the Father to help us regain the ground that we have given up when we held onto those offenses and give us wisdom to deal with whatever the situation is. But most importantly, heal now the wounded places not only in my soul, but in my memory so that I can look back on them realistically, knowing that you have healed me and by acknowledging this, I can be whole again.

Time to Release It

I was having a conversation with someone concerning an issue that they were having concerning their breakup, and as I begin to listen to them and observed their behavior, I realized that their problem was deeper than what was being said. Especially when they began to say that they didn't give the person permission to leave them.

I began to tell them that we can't control another person's feelings but respect their decision even when we don't want to accept what we're hearing.

We don't have a right to hold a person hostage with idle threats as a result of their honest feelings because, truthfully speaking, one would be very upset if they believed that they were being deceived.

I began to warn them that their toxic behavior can and will lead them down a wrong path if they don't get to the root of why they feel that they have to have such control over another person's life. Because whatever they were dealing with internally was more than what was at the top surface.

As they began to respond to my statement, they began to acknowledge that they had rejection issues as well as abandonment issues from their childhood and if anyone gave them any form of attention, whether it was abusive or not, that they saw it as love. If the relationship didn't work, just like clockwork those abandonment issues resurfaced and that thing called failure surfaced up once again.

Unfortunately, this is where many people become trapped in their lives, not realizing that, in order for someone to love them they must love themselves and have a oneness with confidence.

One must understand that the actions or the behavior of someone else has no reflection on them. The way a person mistreats someone who has cared for them only shows that the individual have unresolved issues of their own and is in need of restoration themselves.

Someone defined wholeness as the concept that we contain all potentials for any actions, thoughts, or energy. Wholeness is coming to terms with the acknowledgement of things for what they really are.

We know that we cannot repress or ignore the things that we are confronted with, but instead we must create a peaceful environment as well as constructive relationships because we intuit that these things have something to contribute to our wholeness.

We must come to terms even if the conditions are disturbing that we do not deny any aspect of ourselves even when we make mistakes while learning how to perform effectively.

When a person reaches that point of wholeness, now freedom steps in as one finding more of an inner peace and the spiritual power to become more of the person that they were meant to be and at peace in a singleness of spirit.

Chapter Eight

After the Storm Is Over

Have you ever spent an afternoon in the backyard barbequing or just enjoying a beautiful day when suddenly you notice that everything goes quiet? And after a few moments, you feel a change in the air and out of nowhere, a line of clouds ominously appears on the horizon and now here comes the rain. It's sort of like the calm before the storm where there is a period of peace and without warning, here comes a crisis like turbulence and now life appears to be turned upside down and the type of storm it is will determine the outcome of damages that it produces.

It's like getting a call that your loved one has been in a bad car accident and you're needed at the hospital, and not knowing what to expect brings about anxiety and uneasiness.

Sometimes in life things don't always go smoothly and we are free of stress. Rather than having a sun shiny day, people are stumbling from one crisis to another.

While we may believe that we are the only ones going through turmoil, the truth of the matter is everyone is going through one crisis or another, trying to figure out how to put the flame of fiery darts out.

The same way a storm is any disturbed state of an astronomical body's atmosphere, a crisis doesn't have to be defined as one by those outside your circle to qualify as one. Crises are emotional and physical reactions to some precipitating event or series of events that will disrupt our normal day to day routines that can make one feel overwhelmed and helpless.

If you think your relationship and your reputation are in danger, and it is widely known or acknowledge by your friends or family, here comes the crisis of how one handles it.

Crises by nature are messy, and they stem from unforeseen events. Crises represents turning points in life and in one's reputation, but if handled well, a crisis response can actually enhance ones reputation even though one may have limited control over the events that precipitates a crisis.

Unfortunately, no one can prevent a crisis, but one can choose to have control in the way that they choose to manage the crisis. If one perceives an event as a total and complete disaster from which they can never recover from, they will feel more helpless than ever, forgetting that crises are a normal part of life.

I learned that when the warmer air is displaced upwards, it causes surface air pressure to drop, which creates something of a vacuum effect where the two masses meet. Cold air then rushes in to fill the area of lower air pressure, and this in return forces more warm air upwards.

This starts a cycle of cold air rushing in, pushing the warmer air upward. It is turbulence that causes the storm. This is just like the pressures of life that can go from a peace and calm atmosphere to a heat wave in a minute without warning.

I remember receiving a call from someone who I hadn't seen nor spoken to in years. And I couldn't figure out why they would be calling me. Instead of being patient to find out what the call was all about, I allowed my mind to go in a direction that wasn't making any sense.

My focus was more on the why than seeing that if they were reaching out to me, it had to be important. So I decided to take a moment and stop overwhelming myself with unnecessary imaginations and just listen, and in due time all of my questions would be answered instead of trying to put the cart before the horse without a saddle.

They began to ask me questions that I had no answers to. I began to feel bad about how quickly I reacted to someone who had enough confidence in me to call in spite of how long it had been. I even said to them that I was sorry if I seemed a little apprehensive, and I was very thankful when they said that they didn't receive it like that.

While listening to them, I wondered within myself why in the south in those days did people keep secrets that they knew would eventually come out and lives would be affected or ruined.

Their concern was how is it that everyone around you knew about this deep dark secret concerning a person's life except for the person? How can a loved one deceive you by telling you that you weren't wanted by your mother or father just to find out later in life that those you trusted deceived you?

You talk about a storm that is one because confusion and abandonment, as well as rejection, sets in, and now identity becomes a big issue as rage begins to take control because of that thing called deception, and now here comes a crisis.

I read an article that said understanding the conditions that give rise to powerful storms is the key to preparing for their devastating effects, but the question is: what if you are not prepared? What do you do? Especially when one is developing stomach pain along with confusion while trying to cope, bringing about the inability to concentrate.

It has been said that when dealing with a crisis, one should never withdraw from those who are willing and able to help because those individuals do care. And stay away from those who are bringing more stress. And as hard as it may be, the best way to handle the issue is to not become a part of the problem. But allow the experience to open up to what can be learned and aim at rising above it because how you handle a thing will determine how one survives a thing.

In the game of sports, winning or losing is not only determined by how well the players play, but mainly how well they rebound, especially in basketball. Rebounding is not only in retrieving the ball but how the players and coaches conduct themselves during the game.

If a player or a coach conducts themself in an nonprofessional way and shows unsportsman-like conduct, or shows poor sportsmanship, such as arguing with a referee or by fighting with another player from the opposing team, it can and will break the morale of the team, especially if the team captains don't step in and motivate the players. If there is no regrouping among the players, the result of the impact can be costly.

The player or the coach can be thrown out of the game for their misconduct and the example that they have set, now has an effect on the team, and if they don't shake it off, there will be no regaining or regrouping. Just like in the game of basketball, if we don't conduct ourselves in a proper manner, the affect that we have on someone else's life can be costly just like a bad storm.

How We Handle It

In life, most people try hard to fight against the negative things that are said concerning them, and they try to resist the temptation to retaliate, but when the wrong button is pushed, not only is the person who created the situation in trouble, but everyone that is around at that time will feel the wrath of the effect. And when the innocent remind them by saying they are not the ones who betrayed them, things go from one extreme to the next.

The wrong people are paying for what someone else did or said, and now the cycle begins where excuses start arising like, "I 'm only human, and you don't know what I had to go through." But the thing that is missing is what the individual said; you don't know what they did, not what you did.

Almost all people are treated poorly or mishandled at one time or another, and some don't fully recover from being mistreated. If they are not careful, their lives will be disrupted for many years from their hurtful experiences as they will use negative excuses for irresponsible behaviors.

I realize in life that we sometimes will be tossed like waves and currents that seem so powerful, but I heard a song that said though the storms of life are raging and sometimes it's hard to tell night from day, still that hope that lies within me is reassured as I keep my mind upon the distant shore.

I believe the writer was saying I am going through some difficult times right now, but if I can just see the light at the end of the tunnel and believe that this pain that I am dealing with will soon pass, I know everything is going to be alright. I believe that the writer knew the importance of how we think about the messages that we send out as well as being considerate in how the messages we send affect those people that are around us.

Someone said the best way to handle situations is to not become a part of the problem but allow the experience to open up to what you need to learn and aim at responsibility, honesty, and integrity at all times.

One must not allow those blinders to overshadow them to the point that they forget where they came from because of what one might be going through. For if we forget, the weight will become so heavy that we will not be able to move forward while continuing to make one feel as if they have just stepped into quick sand without a lifeline.

In life, sometimes we lose hope, and it seems impossible to get up, but how you handle your storm will depend upon how you come through it. Disappointments are only failures when you stop fighting and give up. All that matters is how you finish and not how you begin, even when you don't feel that you are handling the situation right because eventually you will get a grip.

Sometimes in life, we lose hope and it seems impossible to get up but how you handle your storm will depend on how well you come through it.

Our twenty sixth President Theodore Roosevelt suffered many storms in his life that would have ruined the best of us. As a young husband, he was pounded by a double tragedy. His mother and wife were stricken by unexpected illnesses, which at first their afflictions did not appear to be serious, but they grew worse, and both died within a few hours of each other on the same day, in the same house, and to make matters worse, Roosevelt's wife had given birth to a daughter only two days before.

Now you talk about a storm, this was one. In life, sometimes one's disappointments will prepare one for their appointment, and this is what our twenty sixth commander and chief did by focusing on his work only three days after his misfortune.

His mind setting was you can't throw in the towel even though it might appear that you're fighting a losing battle because storms don't last long but strong people do in spite of what they go through. Besides, it's not how one starts, but it is definitely how one finishes.

There was a conversation about a man and an old water pump, and it was stated that this man was not only hot from the heat but was very thirsty but couldn't get that old pump to work like he wanted it, so he became frustrated and decided to quit. Those around him explained to him that in order to get something out of that old well, you have to put something in it.

They explained to him that he had to prime that pump in order for it to work because anything worth doing is worth doing poorly until one can learn to do it right. So you see, one must keep pumping because the reward will be great because by knowledge the soul is filled with grace and comforts of the spirit.

You can't focus on the "should have" mentality because no one is exempt from wrong choices and wrong decisions in life. I read in the book of Proverbs that though a righteous man falls seven times, he rises again. As a people, we do fall from time to time and some have been knocked down with blows that have been so devastating that they wonder if they can ever regroup again as a result from the impact.

One must remove those blinders that are showing them their present condition and look ahead like a pilot who is flying through a bad storm and take on the attitude to rise above it and get a clearer view instead of being captured by how bad the storms is because a pessimist sees the difficulty in every opportunity, whereas an optimist sees the opportunity in every difficulty.

And if we can become like the one who is an optimist, we will realize that in spite of how it looks right now, we will weather the storm because we are more than conquers.

"To get something you never had, you have to do something you have never done." When God takes something from your grasp, he's not punishing you but merely opening your hands to receive something better.

We must become like that airplane pilot whose mind setting is, "In order to rise above this storm and come out intact and reach my destination, I must go through it because nothing venture is nothing gained."

You see, "The truth is that our finest moments are most likely to occur when we are feeling deeply uncomfortable, unhappy, or unfulfilled. For it is only in such moments, propelled by our discomfort, that we are likely to step out of our ruts and start searching for different ways or truer answers."

We must keep in mind that yesterday is but a dream, and tomorrow is only a vision. But a today well lived makes every

"In Your Journey Lies Your Awakening"

yesterday a dream of happiness and every tomorrow a day of hope that will allow us to see that even though the storm was the worst ever, one can still come out alright.

Chapter Nine

GETTING PASS THE ROADBLOCKS

When one makes up their mind to get off of one exit and take another that they hadn't traveled, it can lead to roadblocks and detours. Each roadblock or detour has an arrow pointing in the direction in which one must travel. These roadblocks can be very bumpy as well as confusing because of the lack of stability and uncertainty that one must face when switching from one lane of life to another.

Some roadblocks can bring about hesitation and uneasiness when one has to go past things that are familiar such as the shame of their past or look those in the face who criticized and condemned them. But when we are confronted with roadblocks in our lives, we must remind ourselves that roadblocks aren't designed to make one feel like they are box in, but they are actually designed to help one go through the obstacle course that has been placed in front of them.

When one makes the decisions to move away from the thing they believe is weighing them down, they will often find themselves sometimes in the middle of a maze where there seems to be barricades of walls that lead to nowhere.

Those roadblocks of life have blinded one to the point that they can't see the path they should travel because the road map

"In Your Journey Lies Your Awakening"

of life appears to have too many whining turns. Unfamiliar signs that are written in English but reads like Greek leaving one with confusion and doubt as they try and figure out which path is the right one to take as frustration sets in.

Disappointment to disappointment have been in view, and if it wasn't for disappointments there would be no appointments. It's like I heard someone say, "If it wasn't for bad luck, they wouldn't have any luck." This is the way that many feel after years of neglect and setbacks.

Everyone has a right to have these thoughts or feelings for a moment, but one must look realistically at the roadblocks in front of them and ask themselves these important questions, which are: What has beating up yourself cost you? How has being upset and angry most of the time helped you? Or better yet, how has blaming others benefited you?

Many times in life, people get caught up with the idea or facts of how upset and frustrated they are and neglect or fail to see the effect that it has on them, and the toil that it has over their life as habits are developed. You see, habits are like a rope, you add a thread every day until it is impossible to separate or loosen it.

Year after year go by and many people are singing the same old songs with the same ole twist, but it's just a different day. It's like the individual who had too much to drink, and they tell the same old story over and over again until someone says, "That's enough already, change the record and get a new song to sing because this one is worn, old, and has collected enough dust for everybody and their momma."

It's like that old saying, "how dry I am" which is the truth when one repeats and rehashes past events like the drunk asking, "Did I tell you about that story?" They will admit that they did but will automatically go right back to repeating the same thing because that's what's familiar to them.

I'm reminded of a story that I heard concerning a dog on a nail. The question was asked, why is that dog groaning and moaning? Someone replied, "Because he refused to get off of that nail that he is laying on." Someone else said, "Why won't he get up?" And the answer was because he wasn't hurting severely.

The point is when a thing becomes bad enough, there will be some changes made and questions asked on how one can stop this pain from throbbing so that there can be some form of relief. But, due to hesitation and uncertainty, many will continue to believe that a pill is the remedy for the pain, not realizing that some medications are just a temporary relief or an every four hour fix. Some may even think that drinking is the answer to the problem as they fail to realize that drinking can lead to other problems.

Moving Forward

In order to move forward and get past those roadblocks, we must first ask ourselves this very important question: What mental roadblocks are we carrying that are stopping us in our tracks? This can be a challenging thing for most of us because they are hidden well in our minds. Things that one might have heard in their childhood or an experience that was encountered by someone who had a great influence in their life may be the cause.

To unlock that door, one must become like the game we use to play as children that we called "mother may I." One must grant themselves permission to take steps by asking if they are ready to take that step called courage and then develop the courage and believe that they can.

Courage is what it will take in order to step into the next phase of life in order to be set free from those roadblocks of guilt, hurt, and shame. One must keep the idea that roadblocks or detours are designed to keep one from falling deeper in the potholes while the damages are being reconstructed.

There were times when my father would tell me to come by and see him on my lunch break when he was working in an area close by. He was a construction worker who fixed and laid black top on the roads, and I often wondered, why not just patch it up?

But I came to learn that some things need to be torn down and rebuilt because if not, the situation will be worse than it was from the beginning. In life if we don't allow those disappointments to be repaired properly by not covering them up, we will find ourselves in a worse state because we patched up the wound instead of stitching the wound so it could be closed up and healed.

Joseph, who repressed his true feelings toward his brothers, was confronted with a barricade when out of nowhere he had to face which he never dealt with before, finding himself in a situation in which he had to make some serious decisions. At first, those roadblocks of anger set in because his brothers did him an injustice.

He recognized them, but they didn't recognize him, and he spoke to them in a rough manner as he acted like he was a stranger while accusing them of being spies instead of letting them know who he was.

As a result of his bitterness, he had them placed in prison for three days as he played mind games with them. That's how individuals handle their roadblocks in life when they repress past hurts that were never released but concealed for years, while waiting for the right moment to have the upper hand.

Paul the apostle made it clear that he didn't have all the answers, but the one thing he did know was that he was going to forget those things that were behind and press toward what was ahead. Of course, Paul could have reflected back on his past and allowed guilt and shame to overshadow him and cloud his vision of possibilities, but he decided that in spite of yesterday's issues, he would take a chance and step out into his today.

It reminds me of when Dorothy realized that she wasn't in Kansas anymore and saw the obstacles that she had to face. Dorothy could have easily given up and thrown in the towel at the first sign of trouble, but she saw a path and decided to take it.

One must develop and take on that same attitude or mind setting and develop their own GPS system which I call Getting Past the Struggles that's been keeping one down and keep in mind that those who created yesterday's pain in their lives don't control tomorrow's future.

One can't allow themselves to become like fleas that were captured in a jar with a lid on it and couldn't find a way out, so they opt to remain at the bottom of the jar even when the lid was removed and they could get out.

Or become like the elephant who definitely has the strength and ability to break the chains and be free, but because he has been programmed in believing that walking around with a chain around his neck and feet instead of being what he was meant to be, which is free to wander, will accept his fate and remain in that state even when the time comes to be free.

Many people will never press forward in life even if someone gave them the key to unlock the door to their future or gave them a choice to pick either curtain number one or three because of what someone said or did many years ago. We will lose or miss the windows of opportunity because of insecurities they had developed while failing to realize that our finest moments are more likely to occur when we are feeling deeply uncomfortable or unfulfilled.

I read an article once that said it is only in such moments, propelled by our discomfort, that we are likely to step out of our ruts and start searching for different ways to press forward.

Pressing forward means that one must tackle and take charge of the obstacles that's been holding them back and develop that thing called courage.

"In Your Journey Lies Your Awakening"

It has been said, that courage comes when we are in the minority and the test of tolerance comes when we are in the majority. Courage is not the absence of fear, but rather the judgment that something else is more important than fear. As far as failure goes, it is only the opportunity to begin again with more wisdom.

I remember reading about David and Goliath and didn't quite understand why Saul, this great warrior, and his army were afraid to go up against this Goliath person until I read that he wasn't just a champion, but he was intimidating in stature and would make the average person second guess themselves, whether they had what it took to defeat this giant.

That is the same way that some people are who have been broken and put down. A part of them has the desire to move forward, but lack confidence in themselves if they have what it takes to become better than what they were yesterday by not even taking thought on today holds them back.

But this David who was the ridicule by his eldest brother didn't allow anything negative to interfere and discourage him. Even the other men around David tried to discourage him, but David displayed to them that he had that thing called courage and that courage is what makes one confront their obstacles.

I can imagine David asking them where their courage was Or where is there strength in their God? Or better yet, have they forgotten the true meaning of courage? I can imagine David telling them that courage is the quality of the mind that enables us to meet danger and opposition.

Courage has been described as a kind of strength or power to meet scary situations head on. It is called upon whenever one is confronted with a difficult situation such as fear, pain, or something frightening. During this time is when we are confronted with the questions, do we or can we find the courage to face and defeat our fear or will we be defeated by it?

Getting Pass the Roadblocks

In life, when we are striving to do better and move forward from familiarity is when the challenge of what we are equipped with surfaces. We begin second guessing, questioning, and doubting whether we can win the war in our lives that is challenging and overbearing. Encountering our destiny requires strength whether it is in the form of embracing or accepting because courage is required in almost every basic human endeavor.

After being denied and made a mockery of by Pharaoh like Moses was, one would have maybe went and sat under a tree and began second guessing themselves whether or not they had the right assignment, but Moses had undeniable aspiration and determination in spite of the challenge that confronted him. He did not allow that barrier of rejection and mockery put him in a standstill, but through it all he faced that giant without intimidation and conquered.

Getting past the roadblocks requires integrity. There is nothing more disturbing than a person who can't distinguish the difference between right and wrong. In spite of what one believes concerning someone else, the truth still remains that while we are pointing our index finger at others, there is a thumb pointing back at us. Moving forward requires us to take a look within one's self and confront the things that so easily upset us.

I remember receiving a private message on facebook concerning a matter that, in all honesty, for the life of me I could not remember or recall the incident. My first response was to react to the situation by confronting the issue, but what disturbed me the most concerning the matter was the person who sent it did not want me to respond to it.

I felt like a person on trial for a crime they didn't commit but was already found guilty. I felt like there was a barrier in front of me that I couldn't get around.

Destroying the Wall of Disappointment

Now this wall of unbelief began to grow in my mind, and the more I pondered it in a negative way, the more disturbed I became because someone was saying something that I felt was questioning my character and integrity. I wasn't given the privilege to address the issue so that if I was at fault I could ask for forgiveness and the matter would be straightened out, but instead I wasn't given that opportunity.

I became so disturbed and upset that I began to talk to some close, trust worthy friends who were present at the time in which this incident was to have taken place.

To my surprise, they were just as surprised concerning the matter as I was, but their advice to me was that they understood how I felt, but the best thing for me to do was give it time. Of course, this was not what I wanted to hear as that wall of uneasiness began to take over, and I became like a person who was attempting to go and face this giant because that thing called "holding my peace" was not working.

I had to realize that integrity and honesty is not simply a matter of personal determination or willpower, but it is when we personally enforce in our own lives that which ultimately can't be enforced.

Most of us, if we took the time to reflect back on some past experience, we will admit how we found ourselves in a situation and couldn't figure out how the heck it happened, but the person made it appear as though you were the problem.

There are some parents who have been supporting their children from preschool and all through high school, getting them out of one mess or another. They are doing the best they can to keep them from going down the wrong path that will lead to trouble only to be accused of everything that has gone wrong in their lives.

Or better yet, what about the spouse that comes home from work just to be confronted with divorce papers after years of sacrifice and hard work because one is having an identity crisis and now after all these years decided that they needed to be liberated and be that person that had been suppressed?

I recall the time when my husband and a few associates decided to venture out into their own business, and everything was going into the business, and all I kept hearing was so many promises as the bills begin to pile up. Knowing that nothing ventured is nothing gained, I decided to be a supporter and not be a dream snatcher. Just in case it did work I didn't want to look like an idiot.

Business was picking up, and they finally got their big break, and my husband was over the sales department. I was excited because all of our hard work and sacrifices were beginning to pay off, or so I thought, only to have all the air let out of the ball.

The money went missing, business partners went missing, and all habit broke loose and the business crumbled. We were left with unbelief and broke. Talk about disappointment, I had it so bad that none of those partners were not only welcomed to my home, I didn't even want their names mentioned around me, and I had to work on forgiving my husband because, at that time, reasoning didn't make sense to me.

Even though I was mad as heck, something within me, maybe that thing called love, had me try to show some sort of compassion toward my husband because this was his dream for the family so I knew he had to be feeling ten times worse than I was.

This was a bad blow for my family, and the pressure was unbelievable for my husband and I because picking up from such a blow like that was the biggest challenge at that time that we had to face as a team. But through all of the madness, I learned this valuable lesson: in life, there will be disappointments, but we can't let the effect of our disappointments set in and overtake us because it will hinder and bury one with self-pity, as that thing called depression will take over, and without warning, fear will conquer and some will never try again be able to accomplish that thing that lies deep within them because of fear of failure.

Disappointments are not designed to detour, us but they are designed to help improve us and allow us to become the individual's that we are destine to be.

The person who invented the washing machine didn't stop trying because of their disappointments when the machine kept getting low approval ratings and things looked dim. They kept at it until they got it to work, and as a result of it, scrub boards became a thing of the past.

I remember reading about Nehemiah in the bible on how he wanted to build back up the wall that was destroyed in Jerusalem. His heart was in the right place, but he had no idea of the roadblocks that he would have to confront.

Roadblocks are not only signs and barricades but people as well. Just examine it when someone attempts to do something different in their lives that they hadn't done before. The first thing that they would hear from a neighbor or friend and even family members is this question, "Are you sure you want to do that? I don't know because it sounds risky or maybe you should reconsider," but the truth of the matter was that the person wasn't asking or looking for their opinion but was merely sharing what was in their mind to do.

In Nehemiah's case, when he expressed to the king what he desired to do, the king was supportive, but this was not the case throughout his journey, and this will not be the case in some of our journeys.

The San-bal-lat Syndrome

In life, when you make up your mind to do better and become better, the last thing on your mind is opposition because one would think that people would be glad to hear the good news that someone is taking up night classes to get a high school diploma or trying to fulfill their dream by working toward a college degree.

But contrary to what one believes, there is going to be a barricade built by people who don't believe, and if it was left up to them, they would have a roadblock covered at every entrance so that one can't get in or out.

When San-bal-lat heard that Nehemiah had accomplished the completion of rebuilding the wall, he became resentful and took action to condemn the good that was done. He began tearing down and fault finding instead of saying, "Even though I didn't think it could to be done, but they did it," he did just the opposite. It would not have been so bad if he would have kept his feelings to himself, but he had to gather up the haters as well.

You see, when we confront the roadblocks in life, we must make sure that we are wearing our seatbelts because the road traveled will be rocky. Those roadblocks called haters will surface. They will gather as if they are having a board meeting, strategizing how to ruin and discredit what was just built.

Part of the strategy is to come up with a plan to convince you that they misjudged your ability and that they are in favor of what you have done and would like to offer their help.

They are hiding behind that mask they are wearing looking for an entrance to infiltrate their deceitfulness. They will even talk to others that are close to you, persuading them to tell you to give them an opportunity, knowing that there plan is to destroy what was accomplished and people like this have what I would label as the San-bal-lat syndrome.

They are like the sculptures that you see in front of some business buildings or in the park that look like real people sitting on a park bench reading a newspaper, but once you get closer to it, you see they look real but they're not real.

Just look at Saul, he was a ruler who became extremely jealous because David was favored by not just God but by

"In Your Journey Lies Your Awakening"

the people as well. His jealousy had him at a point that at every opportunity that he got, he was plotting out how to slay David.

Some would say they don't understand why Saul would want to harm David since David meant him no harm. But the truth of the matter is some people don't have to do anything for others to envy the drive they see in them.

Roadblocks can be dangerous when one is not focused and can cause a three mile backup and bring traffic to a halt by those detours that appear without warnings. Detours which appear without warnings leave many unprepared for the difficulties that lie ahead.

When we see that detour sign, we have no idea how long we have to travel on that road because detours will take you out of your way, make you late, and require a great deal of patience from you.

Detour roads are roads that have not been traveled before, so one must travel with the hope and belief that the road traveled will point them back in the right direction, or one can choose to turn around and go back.

When the children of Israel were faced with that roadblock of uncertainty, they began fault finding and wanted to turn back, but Moses had faith and belief that where they were going was better than where they came from and pressed forward.

Some roadblocks can be very productive because it can give one a clearer view of certain situations just like one of my favorite movies of all times called "Secretariat." When this housewife and mother made the decision to take over her ailing father's business, out of nowhere came the roadblocks.

Those roadblocks of lack of or no experience began to surface as comments of her being only a house wife while partners fought against her because they wanted to take over and keep her out.

This woman, in spite of her lack of horse racing knowledge, went against all the odds by not allowing others to build roadblocks and detours to hinder her, but she took on the challenge with the help of a veteran trainer who believed she could do it even though it was difficult. They found themselves tearing down those roadblocks as they manage to navigate this male dominated business by ultimately fostering the first Triple Crown winner in twenty five years being done by a woman.

Not allowing roadblocks and detours in life to become a stumbling block can change one's scenery and remind one that if every day was sunny without any obstacles, we would lack appreciation of the good things in our lives that we achieve.

Besides, once we get through those roadblocks and detours that life sometimes throws at us, we feel a great sense of accomplishment as well as relief.

Chapter Ten

Don't Count Me Out

In life, many people are faced with things beyond their control. No one makes the decision whether their parents will be rich or poor or the environment in which they will be raised in. And as a result of it, many are looked down on as well as put down not by strangers but by those who claim to love them.

And if these issues aren't handle properly, those negative remarks can and will damage one's character and self-worth before they hit adolescence.

Jabez's mother gave him his name as a result of her anguish and loss. When one is aware of such negativity, many would assume that as a result of this, maybe Jabez would have some issues knowing that he was a product of everything negative during that period of her life.

When one is aware that their mother openly made the statement that they named their son or daughter as a result of their issues, one would think that son or daughter would feel some kind of way, but instead. they take on the mind setting that "I am not them and they are not me," and the path they choose to travel in their lives have no barrens on me because my journey is not dictated by how someone else views me.

Jabez refused to be counted out because some were aware of his family issues as he stayed focused and became more honorable than any of his brethren. His attitude was "I am not a product of my mother's issues, but I am a product of what I choose to do with my life."

And his way of making sure that he wasn't a product of his environment was saying a special prayer asking the God of Israel to keep him from evil and that the hands of God be with him.

I remember as a child having an identity crisis because I was teased and taunted with daddy jokes because of rumors surrounding who my father was. Those who claimed to love me made it difficult for me when I was in there presence; they would make remarks concerning which side of the family I resembled.

You talk about being cruel, they had the audacity to predict my future by statements made directly to me that was supposed to break me as they boosted on how successful my other siblings would become, but as for me, they saw uselessness.

Did this bother me? Absolutely, and as tough as I appeared, I couldn't understand for the life of me how some so called family members could be so heartless and just right out mean. And as a result of it, I've felt like I always had something to prove because as far as I was concerned, failure was not an option.

This worked in some areas, but I made mistakes in other areas because I had difficulty focusing because it appeared that the battle was over before it began.

But I found comfort in music for that entrance was closed to everyone except for me. And as a result of that safety net, I wrote a song called Blue Skies that carried me through those hard days because I was determined that no one, and it didn't matter who it was, was going to count me out.

"In Your Journey Lies Your Awakening"

Sadly to say, many times the accusations and rumors are designed to hurt others, but the wrong people are affected.

Someone has an issue, and instead of dealing with it the right way, they spread these rumors, not even considering the damages they are causing. Unfortunately, they really don't care how damaging a thing could be, but God help them, because all of us must reap what we have sown.

It is like the complaints that people have concerning some religious groups that don't know how to show the younger generations love and respect because of how they were brought up in the church, so everything the young people do is a sin.

It makes one wonder if they ever read the passage that said through love and kindness has the Heavenly Father drawn mankind. Someone said the older generation of saints act like they have been in church all their lives with no short comings at all, but the truth is all have sin and come short of his glory.

For many years, people have been unable to see the sunshine in their lives because of the stigma they carry from words that have wounded them in the past.

That old saying of sticks and stones may break my bones but words will never hurt me was one of the biggest lies ever told. That old eighteen hundred year old article that sticks and stones may break my bones but words or names would never hurt me was a deception like none other.

Even though the statement was designed and made to try to persuade the child victim of name calling to ignore the taunting and refrain from physical retaliation, it doesn't change the fact that words can bring about wounds when used in the wrong context.

There are people who deliberately use their words as weapons with the sole purpose of inflicting as much emotional pain as possible. Someone used slapping as an example to show that inflicting words, in their opinion, was worse than slapping someone even though hitting is wrong.

The point that they were trying to bring out was that a slap may leave a mark or outward scar, but it will eventually go away, but words can penetrate so deep while destroying a person's self-worth.

They use the illustration of how some couples or a spouse, when they are upset, will fight dirty by using words that cut deep, and the heavy ammunition from what they said is so devastating that it leaves them feeling physically assaulted even though the person never lifted a finger against the other person. But, the sad thing concerning the matter is this may seem like a normal interaction to the person who is inflicting this behavior out.

Words spoken by a parent or teacher who says to children that they will never amount to anything or have the capability to succeed is planting a seed that will grow like one planting seeds for a garden. After much watering and pruning, that seed will grow whether it is an apple seed or corn seed because that is what has been planted. This is exactly what happens when people use words as weapons toward someone.

It reminds me of when someone is trying to destroy another's character. They will say all sorts of things that may or not be true concerning an individual. Those lies will become roadblocks that can and will affect others.

It's like being on trial and feeling like you're having a bad dream because you don't have a clue as to what's going on. But just like after a bad storm, a beautiful rainbow will appear and the sun will shine as the strong winds cease. The good news is that all of us have a choice to accept or reject spoken words that have been said toward us or about us.

Of a truth, some people have been dealt a bad hand, but I have come to learn that the darker it is, sometimes the sweeter the victory will be. Someone said that the stars come out at

Night. They shine the brightest because of what it took for them to come forth.

Have you ever taken into consideration why most award's shows are at night instead of the day? Many would say so that everyone can have an opportunity to see it. But, others say because their darkest hours came right before the break of day.

They have sleepless nights and inner strength that they had to continually push forward when no one else could understand and now the time has come for them to shine and come forth like the noonday.

We can make a decision to remain in the mud or get out of the mud. Why? Ask yourself, did you tell yourself that you were nothing? The majority of people would say no. As crazy as that may sound to some, there are times when we need a reality check and to accept the fact that what someone said about me or thinks of me is their problem and not mine.

One must come to a place in their life and acknowledge that, "Yeah, that hurt me." But, I will rise above it because my destiny lies within me. My journey is not according to what some one's philosophy might be toward me.

I remember in my house growing up in that old Pentecostal church, hearing that watching television or going to a movie was unacceptable as we were not allowed to watch television or attend a movie. As I got older and was able to make my choices, I watched a Disney program or show called Cinderella.

What I admired about it, was how Cinderella, in spite of her mistreatment by her stepmother and sisters, was always imagining herself being at the ball having that dance with the prince even though she was counted out. I wondered if the writer of the movie ever read the scripture in the bible concerning the seven sons of Jesse.

It was stated that the Prophet Samuel visited Jesse's house because he was to anoint the next king of Jerusalem, but because David was ruddy looking and tended sheep, he was overlooked by his father who showed the prophet his other Sons. And even though they might have had the looks and skills, they weren't chosen for the test because how many of us know that a person can look good on the outside but their inside is a mess.

I have heard that one should never judge a book by its cover because what you see on the outside is totally different when you look inside.

It's like being in high school and certain ones are pointed out to be the the most likely not to succeed. Then you have the most popular kids who seem to get all the glory. For some strange reason, the one who was most likely to fail succeeds and make it big, while the most popular, in many cases, gets lost somewhere in the sauce.

I have, like many others, been accused of having confidence in people that others have counted out because of how it looks at the present as they fail to see the potential in others down the road.

I often wondered if those same people who prejudge others how would they feel if someone labeled them before they got started. But on the flip side, maybe they are so critical because spoken words placed on them that they never recovered from.

Seeing someone else push through the criticism that they couldn't, maybe that thing called jealousy has taken root in them. Like Joseph's family who had jealousy towards him and made it clear that they would never bow down.

Because people count you out doesn't give you the right to count yourself out because it is not a matter of what others think, but it is what you believe about you.

There was a story concerning a man who wanted to be a part of the K-9 unit, but he kept failing the test and after the fourth time, he became the joke of the party because the more he went after it, the more he kept coming up short.

"In Your Journey Lies Your Awakening"

He could have remained angry and gave up especially after all the embarrassment, but his mind setting was, "If it's meant to be, it is up to me." And as a result of him believing that he could be part of that K-9 unit, the day came when he met every qualification and shut up the mouths of gainsayers, winning them on his side as they gave him praise.

I remember going to my youngest son's football game and they were losing so bad that the crowd started rooting for the other team. The first opportunity that was presented, I said to my son before he went to the locker room, "Keep your head up because it is just half time, and there is another half to go."

Of course, my son wasn't in the mood for the mom pep talk. But, after whatever took place in that locker room, my son came out and started playing as if he was in a championship game, motivating his teammates and winning over the crowd. I went to screaming, "That's my son," because when others say you can't, you must fight back and say, "Yes!, I can."

In life, when fair weather people count you out, it is only an opportunity to reflect back and regroup just like that business adventure that my husband was part of. That went south and some people thought they knew all the answers without suggestions while spreading rumors about stuff they didn't have a clue about. But, we kept the mind setting like that little train who believe that he could and did.

Life is like a whining turn that goes from one point to another as the doors of opportunity will come back around. If one takes on the mind setting like I read in the bible concerning "I can do all things through Christ who strengthen me," failure would not be an option but an opportunity.

Chapter Eleven

REMOVE THE MASK; IT'S MORNING

While doing some work on my lap top, I notice this advertisement for wrinkle cream kept appearing. At first it was annoying because I would click it off, and here it comes again, but then I decided to take a moment and see what all the hype was about. And as I read the literature, it explained how these creams are designed to eradicate part of the surface skin and after that allow original skin cells to form.

But what really caught my attention is when I read that some wrinkle products don't work at all. The quandary is because some of the ingredients in the cream, while providing moisturizing or other benefits, don't actually address the problem of wrinkles. This in return can be very frustrating and disappointing for those who are expecting wrinkle reducing benefits.

As I began to ponder on what I had just learned, it dawned on me that many of us have received wrong information on how to handle those who have brought such agony and pain in our lives.

Wrong ingredients have been planted in our thoughts, and instead of us seeing what we can become when we release life disappointments, we continue to see through those old lenses

"In Your Journey Lies Your Awakening"

that reminds us of all those yesterday blues as the residue builds up instead of peeling it away.

How ironic is it that we can acknowledge that we need to dial 911 because of some unfamiliar pain in the body that is alarming and there is a need for a medic, but one can't see the warning signs in their lives that they are still allowing the pain from time past to keep them in agony. Or better yet, how is it that one can give advice to others on the grounds of how they see them or allow other people to mistreat them but can't apply that same advice to themselves.

It is a known fact that as a result of untreated disappointments of neglect and pain from a parent, ex-lover, best friend, or children, it can bring about depression, alcoholism, and drug abuse including mental health as a result of life challenges.

Due to many mishaps and unwelcomed experiences, many will fall and find themselves in a trap like a story I not too long ago heard concerning an experiment done with these three monkeys. It was stated that there was a string tied to these bananas at the top of the tree and all they had to do was climb and retrieve them.

Now, the problem wasn't that they couldn't retrieve those bananas, but every time they climbed, another monkey would knock them out of the way until the monkeys just gave up and stopped trying. Unfortunately, these monkeys allowed others to determine their destiny as well as their potential by not realizing that they are equipped with the ability to rise to the occasion.

This scenario concerning the monkeys can be applied to everyday life, especially when one will allow others to continue to entrap them with those yesterday blues.

Finding and allowing one to succumb to what is being spoken instead of realizing that yesterday is over now and today is a brighter day will cause them to forget how hard it was for them to start releasing those pounds of who done what to them or how it happened. They will find themselves right back at the beginning of a bad chapter as a result of allowing others to continue pulling them down.

Sometimes I wonder if maybe those who keep reminding us of why we shouldn't give those a second chance who let us down, maybe they are dealing with unresolved issues that they never recovered from.

Maybe they are hiding behind that ole mask that says misery loves company while believing that others should be just like them by not releasing that ole song that they are still singing that continues to bring back bad memories while failing to realize or see the damage that they are continuing to do to themselves.

There comes a time when a decision has to be made to either let that tooth keep on aching with discomfort and pain or man up and make that appointment to get rid of the problem that is causing the pain.

In order to find relief, one must step out in faith little by little because if the situation is never dealt with, infections will develop and now the issue escalates as one decides to stay in a familiar state that is unhealthy.

Unresolved disappointments that have not been handled properly will grow and spread like wild flowers and trying to figure out where it begins in order to start the pruning process appears to be hopeless.

It's like one being on trial for a crime they didn't commit and their attorney is trying to tell them to be patient, that they have the evidence to prove their innocence. But instead of listening to their attorney, they will begin listening to those who don't have a clue concerning the matter but have all authority concerning an issue that they know nothing about, leaving one questioning and doubting whether or not they will be set free as the result of what others are saying in thier ears instead of hearing from the one who know.

That mask of uncertainties has had many living their lives behind false pretences, but it is now time to get the right cream and start peeling away the pain of yesterday that has had many wrapped up and tangled up and unable to move forward as a result of continuing to play that old song that continues to bring back memories that always have a beginning but no ending.

If one could only imagine the experience of how it would be when they removed those old outdated lenses that are full of scratches and replace them with a new pair, they will find themselves singing that ole song that says, "I can see clearly now, the hurt is gone, and it's about to be a bright sun shining day."

When the static begins to dissipate and one's view becomes clearer, now those blinder's that have been keeping them in darkness will begin to fade away as daybreak begins. Watching those walls of disappointment crumble at one's feet concerning yesterday's blues no longer exists.

Similar to when fresh water was spilled on the wicked witch, those around her who had been under her bondage experienced a sense of fear for a moment, but all of a sudden, when they realized that their bondage had been vindicated and the residue from her mistreatment was being washed away, it gave them such pureness of happiness that they began to experience a brand new day.

Can you just image how your life will be when that hurt of what he, they, and she did become a thing of the pass and those shackles no longer carry that weight known as depression and anxiety is over?

It's birthing time:

We know that in order for something to be birthed, something had to be first planted. In pregnancy, there is a nine month waiting period before that bundle of joy can arrive. But during that time, there are stages and levels that are taking place preparing for the arrival.

In this first trimester when the pregnancy takes place, things began to affect the body as things that use to taste good become sour and bring about an unsettledness.

It's sort of like when individuals are hit with the fact that deception and betrayal has entered the relationship. Now that thing called hurt will bring about a shift in one's chemistry as things begin to change in their atmosphere as morning sickness begins to settle in because the taste is no longer familiar but unpleasant.

As time goes on, unexpected things never experienced before come into play, and how to handle the unexpected becomes tedious as frustration enters in. Not knowing what to do or how to adapt to this new experience can bring about uncertainty as things that were familiar shift in another direction with questions that have no answers.

Those questions and thoughts of how could they, or why did they, begin to grow, and as time goes on, those pounds become a bit much to carry as unstableness sets in.

This period of uncertainty can be uncomfortable causing symptoms like tension and uneasiness as doubt sets in due to the duration of time as things began to form and develop, and the way we handle the situation is what will determine whether the birth be deformed or whether it will be a healthy one.

For we know that if one doesn't do the proper things during pregnancy, all sorts of complication can and will develop due to lack of proper nutrition as one who neglects the reality of a thing as a crisis takes over and creates circumstance beyond one's control. How ironic this may sound, but when one is not careful, they will develop a pattern of past misfortunes and repeat some of the same habits over the same things from their past. What I mean is when the opportunity

"In Your Journey Lies Your Awakening"

comes to receive a fresh start, we have to be watchful of those stumbling blocks from name callers.

This is similar to the pregnancy of a new mother, who may face uneasiness because her experience is unfamiliar as doubt begins to surface concerning whether or not she can endure this new experience as thoughts of uncertainties begin to run rapid in her mind as the sense of urgency to deliver this load becomes inevitable.

In life, everything has a due date whether one is prepared or not. This is similar to that mother who must face that mile stone when the time comes for her deliver. She has no say so or control when that water bag will break and that baby gets in position to leave what has been familiar as he enters into the practical. Now the time has come to push, but the question to you is are you ready to push the weight of disappointments out of your life or will you continue to carry it as a still born?

Or will you develop childlike faith and accept the fact that it is time to release it and let it go or better yet, will you become like the child who wet his bed, got up, and put dry clothes on just to return back and lay in the spot that is still wet?

But now that the baby is in position, the doctor will tell the mother to push because all that she has gone through is about to be over and pure joy will follow, and all that she has encountered becomes just a memory.

For many years, many have been holding on to tight to unnecessary weight, but it is time to push out anger, bitterness, hurt, and pain that has been attached to one's hip for far too long, allowing weeks to turn into months and years. But now the time has come to be like the woman who was ready to deliver that baby and experience the joy and the presence of peace that "releasing will bring."

Oh, the joy and presence of peace that has been locked down and locked up for so long will bring about a release as tears of joy and not pain will flow like a never before experience of peace.

Just imagine how Job felt when his deliverance came after he prayed for his enemies who did him wrong. The bible tells us that the lord turned the captivity of Job when he prayed for his friends and gave him twice as much as he had before. Or better yet, how Joseph was able to forgive his brothers who just did him dirty.

I know some of us have been worse than mishandled, but how many of us have the testimony that our brothers literally sold us to strangers and lied that we were dead or served time for a crime that we didn't commit?

But Joseph, in spite of his pain, was able to forgive his family with all honesty and sincerity. And as a result of Joseph's heart, he was not only blessed with wealth but developed such an inner peace that he not only forgave his brothers, he blessed them and became the better person as a result of not allowing himself to be controlled by yesterday's mishaps.

Now I ask you, aren't you tired of hurting and missing out on the best days of your life as a result of others? Just tensed and stressed out and aging before your time due to stress and mess that you have no control of.

Now is the time to be released from being a hostage to old pains that has one in a place of custody, not realizing that the gates of freedom are awaiting them if they would just pick themselves up and dust themselves off because the key of wholeness lies within one's self, similar to when Dorothy realized that all she had to do was believe because the only one who was hindering her from her destiny was her.

Strong holds are filled with nothing but pain and regrets as a result of someone else's ignorance, leaving one feeling totally used and betrayed as they watch the one who hurt them act like they did nothing wrong, just acting so happy and full of themselves as to make one believe that they are having a beautiful day just traveling along singing zip-a-Dee-doo- dah and skipity aye as they move forward. This leaves

"In Your Journey Lies Your Awakening"

---

the one they hurt in a fetal position, moping and rocking back and forth over circumstances that they can't remember where the breakdown began and why it ended as dark clouds rest over their horizon.

Many are continuing to allow that dark cloud to linger on as they sit moping and lying to themselves and finding excuses to hold on to a corpse that no longer exists. It reminds me of a passage that I read concerning a fig tree. It was stated that this man had a fig tree planted in his vineyard, and for three years, he came looking to get fruit off of that tree only to realize that there was none. As much as he wanted to hold on to that tree, he was confronted with making a decision to either hold on to it or let it go.

There comes a time in everyone's life that, after much crying and agonizing over what one can't have or repair, it's decision making time, because why should one continue to allow those thorns to grow like weeds while smothering one from the possibilities that await them?

It's time to find the right wrinkle cream and peel away the film that has had one hiding behind a mask and see the star that you really are because it is your birthing time. Nothing you have done or what someone else has done to you can interfere with your morning but you.

The sun is not coming out tomorrow for you because the sun is shining on you today, and your daybreak is now and not later. Can you just imagine that caterpillar that has been down and dragging, but the mask that he was wearing sheds off and now what a beautiful butterfly he is for everyone to see and admire. Just like that caterpillar, you don't have to remain in a shell, but you can face the morning.

You might say, "How do I do that after so many years of everything?" And I would say to you, "When was the last time you believed in yourself worth without guilt? Or when did you stop loving the most important person which is you, or better yet, don't you think the time has come to stop seeing yourself like others do, but see the greatness that lies within you?"

Truthfully speaking, how you see you is how others see you, too. You must wash away that old mask by seeing yourself in a different light by using the words of one of my favorite old songs that I still like and love which is, "Good morning, heartache, what's new, but I change the words to say good morning heartache, we are through."

I remember my husband having some unresolved issues with his father, and every time he would try to move forward, there was always this roadblock that kept getting in his way. This continued until one day when he became confronted with a similar situation while helping someone else deal with their family issue that was almost identical to his.

Whatever took place had my husband to the point of telling me that he needed to take a trip home and get things right and would I join him? I would not have missed this moment for the world because I have been telling him for years to iron things out. I was just grateful to say the least for the eye opening experience that had him ready to confront the issue. It has been said that there is a time and season for all things, and ours had finally arrived.

When my husband and I arrived in his hometown, we stayed a few nights at the hotel before heading to see my father-in-law. The ride was quiet, but my husband would glance at me every few minutes asking me was I alright, opening up that door for me to encourage him because I could tell he was a bit nervous.

After arriving, I quietly whispered to my husband that everything is going to be alright. And what an experience it was when the both of them began to speak. I sat there in amazement as my soon to be eighty year old father–in-law begin to say that he had been longing for this moment for many years.

Watching a seasoned man become so humble was overwhelming because he could have reacted like many from that old school that would have made it clear that, "I'm your father and I don't have to explain nothing, nor give you an explanation," but instead he set the example that even a father can say, "I made a mistake," and, "Can you forgive me?"

The respect they showed toward one another as they spoke to each other was moving, and watching my husband turned in to a little boy was a bit much, especially when he began to say daddy. I could only wish that my oldest son was with us to witness this revelation because my husband would have a fit because our son still says daddy instead of dad, but I guess I could say safely that my husband was experiencing that father and son moment.

Later that evening, we decided to stay over, and it was as if I was in another place in time because watching the two of them together was incredible. And as I sat there, I realized for the first time that not only does ever boy need a hero, but every man needs a father to look up to.

Seeing the type of father-in-law that I have was a wow moment for me because it takes a real man to own up to his responsibilities without excuses. What a birthing that was for me just to watch them remove that film of the past and rid that residue that had been leaving nothing but stains being flushed away.

Watching my husband and his father rekindle something that was on the back burner reminded me of an article that I read that said, "Until the pain of being the same is greater than the pain of change, there will be no change." When one begins to get in touch with their purpose, it is safe to say that their destiny is not far behind.

The psalm tells us that our trust should be in the shadow of our heavenly father's wings because that's where we can make refuge, but if we are inflexible in our expectations of how God should work, we can run into trouble. When the earth seems to move under us, let's be flexible in our expectations but firmly confident in our heavenly father's steadfastness.

Now that we are coming to the close of the pages of this book together, allow me to be the first to say good morning to your new beginning. I pray that my sharing with you brings about happiness in your life that has been screaming to come out. My hope is that after mediating on what was written, you find yourselves walking in a never before place of fulfillment and peace.

Keep in mind that while you are transitioning out of your old season into the new, there will be some tests, but don't allow yourself to be fearful because as you transition from one point in life to another, many changes will take place as you begin to rid out of your life unnecessary weight that has been a sore thumb as well as people that don't mean you any good.

Remain vigilant while entering your new season as you learn from yesterday's mishaps and mistakes. Remain true within thyself because no one can determine your destiny but you.

Keep this prayer before you because I know it will be a blessing to you as it has been for me time after time:

Father God, as an act of my will, I choose to forgive any and everybody who has brought pain and caused me harm in one way or another. Father, I not only forgive them, but I am asking you to forgive them, too and don't hold anything to their charge but to their ignorance.

If there is anything remaining in me that is not good toward anyone, I ask that you remove it away from me. I ask that you help me to rebuild the things that I have lost as a result of those offences and give me the knowledge or wisdom to properly handle any occurrence that might resurface.

Father, please heal those wounds that have been placed in my soul as well as in my memory and allow me to see them through the eyes of forgiveness as you have forgiven me more times than I can imagine.

Father, I thank you for letting me know that your joy is my strength and that there is nothing too hard for you and that you love us in spite of ourselves.

And from a personal note, even I ask anyone who might be reading this book that I offended and have not given an apology to or may not be aware of the offence to please forgive me as I have already forgiven you.

About Dr. Shirley M. Gaines

*P*astor, author, motivated speaker, teacher, worship leader, entrepreneur, wife, & mother of two. These are all the hats that Dr. Shirley M. Gaines has successfully adorned throughout her journey. Dr. Shirley M. Gaines has been honored and praised for her spiritual leadership & counseling by her congregation, community, & other Pastoral Leaders on a global scale. Dr. Shirley M. Gaines was ordained as a Pastor in 2005. She earned a doctorate in Clinical Religious Counseling. She is recognized as an authority in the field of spiritual counseling and healing in every aspect of life. Her works have been acknowledged as ground breaking. During her 32 years of experience, she has pioneered and refined a highly effective way that one can experience a self intervention technique called the "Journey of Awakening".

Dr. Shirley's works and teachings have been inspired by her own personal healing journey back to complete health. In 2008 she found herself drifting into depression after years of emotional abuse from family, friends & so-called believers. She knew she had to get her affairs in order on a spiritual, emotional and mental level or she would die at an early age.

She revisited that place in her heart where she lacked faith and confidence in God. She increased her personal time with God and asked him to forgive her for anything she have done to others, forgive others for mistreating her, & most of all, forgive her for detaching herself from Him. Her heart's desire was for God to make her whole once again. She allowed God to take complete control of her life and every oppressing situation in it. It was a process...however, 3 years later, she awakened. The journey she took progressed her to a point of recovery and cured her of all hatred and bitterness.

"Journey of Awakening", Dr. Shirley's method for whole body transformation enables individuals to use their own life experiences to achieve remarkable results thru simple techniques and mind changing attitudes that revitalize the soul from within. In addition to her book "In Your Journey Lies Your Awakening" and the supporting Workbook "Journey of Awakening" she, together with her husband Bishop Dr. Sidney L. Gaines, operates a national healing clinic to help you fulfill your destiny of living on divine purpose. Her innovative approach to addiction, prevention and education has brought her to the national platform once again.

Dr. Shirley M. Gaines resides in Central New Jersey with her best friend and husband, Bishop Dr. Sidney L. Gaines. She enjoys sharing her personal story and describing the profound healing techniques which have impacted her life and the lives of so many others. Her lectures, workshops, and one-on-one counseling nationally and internationally is designed to support others in generating their own healing and allow optimum health and well-being in all aspects of their lives.

Very Special Thanks

To my niece Irene and my nephew Jay who took the time to give me great encouragement and drive concerning this project from day one, I love you and value your trust and respect that you have for me.

Evangelist Pauline Powell who gave me permission to share her experience on how she went from smoking packs of cigarettes a day to going cold turkey overnight, and even though I didn't put it in this assignment, I really appreciate it, but on second thought, mentioning it places it in here and thanks for the feedback .

Evangelist Joyce Water, thank you for your prayers, belief, and excitement concerning this assignment. I appreciate all your concerns and thoughtfulness toward me during the working of this assignment, and my prayer is that this project brings about everything you thought it would.

Lisa, my sister in law who allowed me to take over her dining room table with all my papers and for letting me read to her every time an opportunity was presented.

My oldest sister, Frances, who encouraged me and wouldn't let up until I completed this project, and I thank you whole heartedly for allowing me to share some of your experiences in this project. I love you, and I'm grateful and honored that you are my sister, much love always.

To my youngest sister Teresa who has always believed in me and loved me, I love you even though I didn't use your title and you know why (smile), but you are the best, and I appreciate you just as much as you appreciate me.

Much love and respect to two special people, Carneil and Tisa Brooks, I thank you from the bottom of my heart for not just seeing but believing in the message.

Bishop Roosevelt and Pastor Myrna Johnson, I thank you for being my mentors, spiritual advisors, parents in the gospel, friend, but most importantly, I thank you both for loving me down through the years.

Doctors Samuel O. and Katie M. Kirkland of Shepherd's Care College, continual blessings for all that you do in making a difference in many people's lives including mine.

My mother, Reverend Helen G., who drug us to church night and day and day and night, I really appreciate and value the sacrifices you made for us eight children down through the years. I thank you for my spiritual up bringing because it has made me the woman I am today, and I thank God for you.

Last but not least, my two sons Thomas and Tyrone whom I thank God for. Words could never express how much I value and love the both of you. And my prayer is that one day the both of you will experience the same love for your children when they arrive as I feel toward the both of you. And I thank the both of you for the love and respect that you young men have and still show me till this day. What an honor and experience I have received from the both of you as well.

I saved the best for last, my wonderful husband Doctor Sidney L. Gaines (Bishop) who has really and truly loved and respected me for over thirty years and counting. I appreciate the confidence and support that you have given me while working on this assignment, along with the sub-title. I thank you for not allowing me to quit when I wanted to. I thank God for how you have been that example down through the years for our children and the values that you have placed in them. You are simply the best and I love you, and the next thirty will be better than the first thirty,

Your one and only wife.

CONTACT THE AUTHOR

For more information about Dr. Shirley M. Gaines and her speaking and book signing events, please visit:

www.journeyofawakening.org

Speaking Engagement:

Contact: "Journey of Awakening"

@ 609-281-5268

E-mail:dr.shirleymg@gmail.com